C

Weave a joyful

Nadine Sanders

Theme & Variation

More *Weaving that Sings*

Theme & Variation

More *Weaving that Sings*

by Nadine Sanders and Joyce Harter

designed and edited by Lucy Brusic
photography by Kim Sheagren
illustrated by Marie Westerman

The Singing Weaver, Chehalis, Washington

Parts of this book have previously appeared as *Weaving that Sings* by Joyce Harter and Nadine Sanders (Loomis Studio: Northfield, MN, 1994).

Library of Congress Catalog Card Number 2002091782

ISBN 0-9720248-1-6

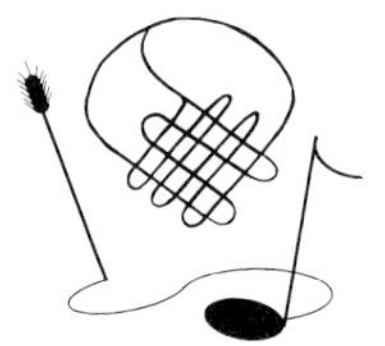

The Singing Weaver
Box 268
Chehalis Washington 98532
Tel: (360) 740-0914
Fax: (360) 740-5517
http://www.singingweaver.com

Printed by Sexton Printing, St. Paul, Minnesota

This book is dedicated to Carrie Aadland
without whose listening ear
and constant support of my work,
this book would not be.

Table of Contents

Foreword

IN THE YEARS since Theo died I have given a number of talks, mainly to weavers guilds, concerning the enriching legacy she has left us, of her approach and development of weaving as an art form (which indeed is the title of her book published in 1975), and of her personality and beliefs. Much has been written about her by many eminent artists from different parts of the world. Some of these are to be found in the most excellent of biographical works, published by the University Gallery, Leeds. in 1992, *Theo Moorman 1907-1990: Her Life and Work as an Artist Weaver*, compiled by Hilary Diaper.

Because she has been so instrumental in my growing appreciation of art expressed in the medium of weave, and instilled in me a deeper understanding of how the search for inspiration can evolve from say, "photographic-like observation to an inner consciousness, an 'abstraction,' when the 'seeing eye' has given a deeper image and whole new dimension"; and because she required of me to become a trustee of the Charitable Trust she intended should come into operation after her death, I wish to quote from her own writings in which she expounded her belief in the importance of the fusion of art and craft. Theo writes, "My own desire is to express and perhaps communicate something of my response to my environment through my craft. I am concerned with producing an abstraction from a visual experience rather than a true abstract. This abstraction can deviate so far from the original literal image as to be unrecognizable but still retain something of the primary vision and impulse." She also wrote in an article headed "Fifty years of weaving," "I have become increasingly aware that simplicity and meaning can go hand in hand." She also says, "It is sad that it takes so long to learn to be simple, to recognize and accept what is given to us through our materials and our technique. A deep respect for the beauty of these elements and the importance of fine technique and attention to detail, are major parts of our equipment." She was primarily addressing weavers, but it surely is relevant in many fields of life and I consider these utterances to be quite profound.

She came to be known and loved the world over and made many deep and abiding friendships. She had a delightful down-to-earthness about her, a lovely sense of humour, and yet a rocklike strength of character, combined with both sensitivity and perception. Moreover she courageously maintained an admirable self-discipline through to the end of her life. Her works are to be found in many churches and cathedrals and in innumerable homes throughout the United States, New Zealand and of course throughout the United Kingdom.

Eileen Chadwick
Trustee of the Theo Moorman Charitable Trust
Somerset, England

Acknowledgments

The author of a book is simply a person who puts together many different thoughts and ideas with a lot of help from many other people. These are the people who helped me and what I thank them for.

Joyce Harter, my mentor and friend, for co-authoring;

Lucy Brusic, for editing, visioning, and modeling;

Dan Jorgenson, my boss, and David Wee and the other English professors at St. Olaf College who taught me how to write;

Kim Sheagren, for photographing all the new work;

Amy Niemann, and Kris Olson, for modeling;

Adam Brusic, for scanning many strange objects and preparing the digital color for publication;

Andrew Grove, for technical support and CD-ROM design;

Kara Johndro, Norma Ames, Deb Brandon, Peter Horsfall, Barbara Viehman, and Fritzi Galley for contributing to the book;

Eileen Chadwick and Deborah Elliott for contributing words and images of Theo Moorman;

Lana Schneider, Sharon Tessman Hoiland, Don and Barbara Berg for reading the manuscript;

Laura Fry and Chris Lunn, who believe in the music of Straw Into Gold and the Singing Weaver enough to help promote my work;

Valerie Doyle, my administrative assistant;

Carrie Johnson, who keeps me going to the gym;

LeRoy and Ellen Sanders, my parents, who are the only people I know who work as hard as I do but never complain;

The leadership of the Minnesota 4-H program which provided me with an education just as valuable as academic learning;

Professors at the Oregon School of Arts and Crafts from 1990-1993;

The participants in the Weaving Digest online community who answered my questions;

Weaving guilds and organizations throughout the United States and Canada for contracting with me to present programs and teach workshops;

The weavers who have been my students and my teachers.

Of course, none of these gracious people is responsible for any errors that may show up in the text. I accept responsibility for any that remain.

Authors' Introduction

SINCE THE ORIGINAL version of *Weaving That Sings: Variations on the Theo Moorman Technique* was published in 1994, both Nadine and Joyce have continued to experiment with this technique. Joyce works prolifically in her home studio creating one-of-a-kind clothing, wall hangings that make personal statements, and home furnishing pieces. Nadine teaches across the country gleaning insight and inspiration from students who are seeing the technique with new eyes. *Theme & Variation: More Weaving That Sings* keeps the best of the original book—weaving exercises, succinct directions, clear drawings, technical tips but adds greater emphasis on designing for the weave structure, new uses of materials such as fabric as weft and new applications of the double-warp overlay technique. The color photography throughout the book showcases the work of the two authors from 1993 to 2002. This book includes a CD-ROM. Printable drafts and exercises, video clips of technique and audio clips of woven harmonies performed by Nadine's ensemble, Straw Into Gold, expand upon the written concepts and woven work in the book. Digital images of additional work by the authors and other weavers, and hyperlinks to resources will keep the book updated.

Joyce Harter

I was a potter before I was a weaver. In reading about pottery in the southwestern United States, I discovered a maxim that Native American potters used as they shaped their beautiful vessels. When the shape was pleasing and the form just right, the potter would say, "That pot sings."

The idea that a woven work could also sing stayed with me as I gradually shifted to a career in weaving. When a woven design works perfectly, with the yarns from which it is made, to create a piece that can be no other way, then we can speak of weaving that sings. Design and yarn can work together harmoniously in the Theo Moorman technique. This weave, named for the woman who developed it, is an adaptation of plain weave to create tapestry-like woven effects.

My introduction to Theo Moorman's work came in the early 1970s with a slide lecture presented by a friend of hers. At that time I was already involved in weaving for churches. I was interested in the use of graphic design for the various needs of the clergy and the church. I felt very strongly that design and symbols should be easily visible from the back of the church.

I had first developed a method of placing embroidery on handwoven cloth without having to mark on the cloth. I wove a section of cloth, then sewed down a design drawn on interfacing, outlining where the embroidery should be. I cut away the extra interfacing and embroidered the design areas using a *colcha** stitch. This technique allowed for large areas of designed images but was very time consuming. This process was, nonetheless, a forerunner to my adopting the Theo Moorman technique.

After viewing the slides of Theo Moorman's work, and reading her book, *Weaving as an Art Form*, I saw that I had found the medium to combine weaving with my interest as a graphic artist. The Moorman technique, which permitted flowing areas of color, lines that could be thick or thin, and mixed colors on the surface of the cloth, met my specifications. It might be said that, whereas Theo Moorman moved in the direction of structural diversity as she continued to weave, I moved in the direction of greater graphic possibilities. To this end, I developed special methods for creating layered and textured designs.

When I began to work with the Moorman weave, I was using a heavy rayon yarn; I liked this yarn because the weight of the finished cloth elimi-

**Colcha* means coverlet or quilt; the stitch is found on embroidered bedspreads in the American southwest.

nated the need for lining. In order to continue to use this yarn, I reduced the number of ends per inch and changed the sleying order. In addition, I used a fine metallic gimp for tie-down warp because it was appropriate for all the seasons of the church year.

Although Theo Moorman suggested several variations of her technique (many of them related to the spacing of the tie-down threads), she questioned my use of a gold tie-down when I showed my work at the Philadelphia Handweavers' Guild exhibit where she was a juror. I, however, have found it a useful variation and have continued to use it along with fine cottons in a variety of colors. Through the years I have used other yarns such as wool and wool/rayon for the ground warp with a matching tie-down color.

Liturgical weaving business

Some church denominations use symbolism, cloth, and colors associated with the church year as part of the worship experience. This weave structure was a cost-effective way to produce such work for the church. The Theo Moorman technique became the basis for my 26-year cottage industry in weaving clergy stoles and altar hangings for churches.

I found a market for contemporary handwoven work in churches and began my business to fill the orders. In the late 1970s, moving from the east to the midwest diversified my audience. My Moorman-style hangings related to small rural Midwestern churches, some very old, just as Theo's work in the British Isles related to the cathedrals of England. In addition, the 1970s were a time of revival of interest in handcrafted work. Women were being ordained and needed clergy stoles designed for them. One satisfied parish or clergy person would inevitably lead to another order for this style of handwoven work.

Under the business name of Joyce Harter Weavers, my liturgical weaving business expanded to include a team of subcontractors. Many of my commissions are still in use in churches across the United States and several foreign countries. Designing for this weave was particularly satisfying for me as I continued to explore ways to use it. Over these years, I produced six hundred clergy stoles, three hundred sets of paraments, and one hundred wall hangings in the Theo Moorman technique.

Barbara Berg came to work with me in the 1980s as an associate. In 1993, I sold the business to her. The name of the business is now "I Weave What I Believe," a closing I often used when corresponding with parish pastors. She continues to produce work in the same technique and sometimes I weave a liturgical piece for her.

Since the publication in 1994 of *Weaving That Sings: Variations on the Theo Moorman Technique*, my work has focused on using the Moorman technique in rugs and clothing with a variety of yarns. Additionally, using commercial cloth both as a basis for Moorman-type designs and as a background for such designs has captured my attention. The Moorman weave is a versatile weave; I continue to explore it as the form of weaving that can best express my design abilities. Although I have passed the torch of teaching to Nadine, I occasionally present this technique to new weavers. I watch with joy the adaptations of the Moorman weave that take place when students see its possibilities.

Joyce Harter
March 2002

Nadine Sanders

I have worked with my hands since I was a child. When I first met Joyce Harter, my background was in sewing and quilting. Although I lived on a farm, I didn't know anyone who raised sheep or spun wool. The only weavings I had seen were rag rugs my grandmother had commissioned from her old clothing. Yet when I walked into Joyce's studio, I felt that weaving somehow seemed familiar. The whoosh of the shuttle and thud of the beater sounded like music.

I liked what I saw and heard in Joyce's studio and wanted to learn to weave. For several years during college I did promotional work for Joyce's liturgical weaving business. But after college I worked in a field that didn't satisfy the need to create with my hands. I finally made the decision to enter art school. I took all the required fine arts classes and weaving courses. When the inlay quarter came around, I was ready to dive into the Moorman technique. I did all of the exercises in *Weaving as an Art Form* and I was hooked.

Immediately I started thinking of all the different materials I could inlay. In my surface design and dyeing classes, I experimented with painted ground warps and saw the potential for ikat and dye-painting yarn, paper, and fabrics to be used with this structure. At first, materials drove my interest in this technique. As I've matured as a weaver, I have come to appreciate the eclectic approach this structure allows.

When *Weaving That Sings: Variations on the Theo Moorman Technique* was published in 1994, I had graduated from art school and was finding my way in the weaving world. The book determined my path as teacher. Teaching the Moorman technique and designing for the technique at workshops and conferences just generates more ideas. I tell my students I must teach this so they can weave and expand upon the ideas I will never get to; in turn, their work and their questions fan my curiosity and my desire to explore directions I hadn't previously considered.

My weaving professor told me that he was spending his life focusing on plain weave because there was so much to explore with just that structure. I have come to appreciate the wisdom of his philosophy. There are so many different weaving techniques and patterns that one could spend a lifetime sampling them. A friend has said about me, "You know a little bit about a lot of things and a *lot* about a few things." Theo Moorman is what I have chosen to know and keep learning a *lot* about.

I often ask myself what else can be done with this technique? How else can this technique be used? In 1994 I received a grant from the Olympia, Washington, Handweavers Guild to study variations on the Moorman technique being done by weavers all over the world. As part of that experience, I taught a group of weavers in El Rodeo, Mexico. Most of them were fairly new weavers. Since my Spanish was very basic, a lot of my teaching was done by demonstrating and observing. The spark of exhilaration when those weavers started creating free-form shapes with the pattern inlay yarn drove the point home for me that this technique is very special.

Many weavers, after having tried grid structures on the loom, have an "aha" experience when they discover the Moorman technique. So many say, "This is what I have been looking for to express my ideas in weaving."

Although this book mainly shows new work by Joyce and me, I'm excited about weavers who are also beaders who use beads as pattern inlay. Spinners who want to learn to weave or who are new to weaving are also discovering the Moorman technique. By nature, this structure accommodates a variety of thicknesses and textures of yarn without distorting the background. Since the pattern inlay sits on the surface of the ground, it shows off the sheen, color, and texture of handspun novelty yarns beautifully.

I am the Singing Weaver. The Moorman technique permeates all my life. I use it to weave costumes for the musicians in my group, Straw Into Gold. I weave backdrops and name banners for performances and presentations. I create rugs and wall hangings for shows and commissions, and I make items to sell and barter for goods and services. The link between making music and making weaving continues to ground my actions in the belief that visual and performance arts belong together in a marriage of harmony, texture, rhythm, color and design.

I was a writer before I was a weaver. This book is a collaboration of two friends—one who weaves all the time and one who teaches all the time. Joyce and I have created this book together. Joyce wove much of the new work appearing in this book and wrote the bulk of chapter eight. I wrote the remaining chapters. The photos have the authors' initials at the end of the caption to identify the artist.

Nadine Sanders
March 2002

Deborah Elliott

Theo Moorman
1907-1990

Chapter 1

Theo Moorman: Her Life and Work

THEO MOORMAN WAS born in Leeds, England, May 25, 1907. She died January 30, 1990. She remained single her entire life.

Although Theo studied at the Central School of Arts and Crafts in London, she later wrote that her three years of schooling there had been tedious and of little use. She thought her schooling might not have been such a waste if she had at least learned to draw. Only in her weaving classes did she find some contentment, and even there the training in design and aesthctics was minimal. The stress was on craftsmanship; the school was influenced by the Arts and Crafts Movement, which followed from the philosophy of William Morris. Fortunately, Theo's first job out of school—at Heal and Sons, Ltd., a London furniture store—was an important second education in art and design. Here she was apprenticed in a weaving studio and produced contemporary rugs and cushion covers. After two years she boldly moved on to become a free-lance weaver in London. Her curiosity to work with new materials and to explore texture drove this phase of her education.

Several years later her friendship with the manager of Warner and Sons mill led to a job as a weaver/designer developing home furnishings. At Warner and Sons she was exposed to weavers using fine silk to weave fashion fabric for royalty. She not only picked up skills in handling fine yarns but also came to appreciate the refraction of light on silk. The ideas of the Bauhaus, a school founded by Walter Gropius in 1919, greatly influenced her design aesthetic during these formative years. "The awareness of the importance of architectural proportion, of empty space and light and of texture, all seemed to form a link between weaving and the other arts." (28) Theo was always grateful for this period of her life where the confluence of the Morris-inspired practical training and Bauhaus-informed design education laid a foundation for her woven explorations during the last thirty-five years of her life.

If World War II had not occurred, Theo Moorman might have continued to weave fabrics for interior furnishings. However, the war changed the direction of her life. During the early part of the conflict, she designed opaque shutter fabric for a special camera being developed by the British Ministry of Aircraft. Although the camera was never produced, the experience of working with fine threads at 600 ends to the inch gave her confidence that shaped her later work.

In 1943, Theo was appointed to the council for the Encouragement of Music and Arts. In this position she arranged for traveling exhibitions and brought artists in contact with the public. The experience was the catalyst for her transformation from a purely functional to an artistic weaver. She described her exposure to modern art, the artists, and the public during this time as "emerging from a long and dark tunnel into brilliant and glorious daylight." (75) She listed as great influences the work of Henry Moore, Barbara Hepworth, Ben Nicholson, Paul Klee, Mark Rothko, and Richard Smith.

In 1953, when she tried to go back to industrial weaving, she realized that her interest no longer lay in that direction. Her earlier acquired interest in working with fine yarns, and her new appreciation of the arts pointed her in a new direction—toward pictorial weaving. While figuring out how to weave pictorially without the time-consuming labor of tapestry weaving, Theo developed the technique that carries her name. The technique is a variation of plain weave. Her

All quotations in this chapter come from Theo Moorman as quoted by Hilary Diaper, ed., *Theo Moorman 1907-1990 Her Life and Work as an Artist Weaver* (Leeds: University Gallery, 1992). The page number is noted at the end of the quote.

innovation was to differentiate the weight of the warp threads; a heavy warp is threaded on the front shafts (1 and 2); a fine warp, on the back shafts (3 and 4). Woven together (1-3 opposing 2-4) in plain weave, the entire warp produces a firm fabric (the ground). When the fine tie-down warp (shaft 3 or 4) is raised independently, colored shapes can be placed on top of the background cloth, where they are anchored by the tie-down warp.

Theo was always modest about having a technique named after her. She insisted that other weavers, possibly the ancient Peruvians, must have used something similar. Nonetheless, she does appear to have been the first modern weaver to see the possibilities of this adaptation of plain weave.

At first, she was unsure of her ability to design. Her two earliest commissions, liturgical pieces, were produced from drawings by British sculptor Austin Andrew Wright (1911-1987). Eventually, with great hesitation, Theo began to create designs. More than half of her thirty-seven commissioned works were for churches and cathedrals. Theo's abstract approach to design served her well in these commissions. She felt that traditional church pictorial symbols were dead metaphors. So she used more universal forms and shapes—circles, rocks, flames. She took great satisfaction when people responded emotionally or intellectually to her work. Her brother was a bishop in the Anglican church so the connection to liturgical commissions may have seemed natural, but Theo said she was not a religious person. (49) Her joy in the commissions came from the intellectual and creative problem solving of working with architects, committees, and the variety of spatial considerations that churches presented.

In 1975, her book, *Weaving as an Art Form: A Personal Statement*, was published. This book, which is still in print, is a classic in weaving literature whether or not one is interested in the specifics of the Moorman technique. It provides valuable insight for weavers seeking to connect their inner lives with their craft. *Weaving as an Art Form* showed how far Theo had come from the concept of weaving as purely utilitarian. When she was in school in the 1920s, one did not weave wall hangings or art pieces. But Theo found her way to self-expression as an artist by taking her artistic visions and weaving them. Though she felt she did not know how to draw, she made rough sketches from nature and translated those sketches to cloth. Fine threads gave her work an airy, almost transparent quality. When asked why weaving was her chosen medium she responded with an honest practical answer. "I can't paint; I'm no good at it; I never have been any good at it. I just am not a painter or a sculptor, so for me it had to be this way. If I had been able to draw say, like Ben Nicholson, life would all have been much easier." (From a conversation with Edward Robinson) (46)

Theo felt that the sheer variety of materials available to weavers set them apart from other artists. She used high quality yarns, often linen, cotton, rayon, and wool. By blending different fibers and textures she created rich palettes and subtle variations. Always observant of and interested in the natural world, she collected shells and rocks. Not only did their shapes intrigue her but she also drew inspiration from nature's color palette. In later years she included found objects in some of her weavings. "One is involved in a dialogue between the gifts that come from the medium and those emanating from the seeing eye." (86)

She continued to experiment with woven structure even after she stopped doing industrial work. She was well aware of the work of sculptural fiber artists such as Magdalena Abakanowicz, but it was the work of painter Richard Smith in a 1975 exhibition that inspired her intellectually and emotionally to a new phase in her career. To create additional planes on the surface of her work, she invented a fan-shaped reed* to produce bands that widened and narrowed. Then she incorporated these

*Further insight and instructions on building a fan-shaped reed are found on pp. 123-127 *Theo Moorman 1907-1990 Her Life and Work as an Artist Weaver*, of Hilary Diaper, ed., (Leeds: University Gallery,1992).

bands in her hangings. Floating on top of the ground, sometimes being woven back in, gathered, twisted, spiraling—Theo found endless fascination in using these woven strips in her designs. Theo drew her inspiration largely from painters, sculptors, and the work of twentieth-century abstract artists. In the design process she worked out whether her ideas could be expressed with yarns. Respecting the limitations of the weaver's craft was important. She felt very strongly that certain things should not be woven. Overly complicated pictorial designs…"can lead to a forced and tortuous situation which breaks one's sense of rhythm in the work." (30) She believed great artists had to develop poise to process the leaps and pitfalls of creating. "Often I am aware of a sensation of balancing on a knife edge. Surrounded by so many possible pitfalls, there is just a chance of holding one's true course." (55)

Although Theo's weaving career spanned sixty years, it was the last thirty years of her life in Painswick, Gloucestershire, that were the most productive. During this time she published the biographical reflection *Weaving as an Art Form.* She taught workshops in the United Kingdom, the United States, Canada, and New Zealand. She generously shared her insight with students of all levels. Students fondly remember her patient encouragement and her large, capable hands. The blend of commissioned work and the work she created for exhibitions or sold to individuals kept her absorbed in design and weaving. Outside of her liturgical work, she made only wall hangings. Once at a conference in the United States Theo stopped a weaver walking down the hall and asked how the woman's vest was made. The weaver replied that it was the Moorman technique! Theo was astounded as she had not considered this application.

Theo realized how fortunate she had been to have the financial freedom to explore her art form for so many years. She wanted to encourage weavers struggling to work full-time in the profession. In 1985 she set up The Theo Moorman Charitable Trust.

The mission of the trust is to "enable weavers to enjoy artistic freedom in order to contribute to the development of the craft and the education of future craftsmen…" (139) by providing grants for weavers for education, to purchase materials or equipment, and to extend further the field of weaving. From 1991 to 2000 this trust has provided grants to thirty-seven weavers from the United Kingdom.

After her death in 1990, Theo Moorman was commemorated in an exhibition at the University Gallery in Leeds. The exhibition was the occasion for a retrospective volume, *Theo Moorman, 1907-1990: Her Life and Work as an Artist Weaver*, edited by Hilary Diaper. This book contains a list of Theo's exhibitions, some articles she wrote about her work, and tributes by weavers who knew her. In 2001, *A Legacy in Weaving—A Celebration of the first decade of grant-giving by The Theo Moorman Charitable Trust for Weavers* was published. The book features work and statements by the grant recipients.

Theo's was a productive life. The weavings, the books, the photos, the trust fund, and the interest in the technique still endure at the beginning of the twenty-first century. In a hundred years, the name of Theo Moorman may not be recognized nor her technique widely known. Or technology could preserve her written words and her images to inspire generations yet to come. Regardless, I believe her enduring legacy for weavers is the spirit of deep exploration in one area of interest and her desire and ability to share her knowledge freely with others.

"The starting point of all that I hold to be significant lies in the bold assumption that as weavers we have in our hands the unique components of a work of art."—Theo Moorman (From the first chapter of a book Theo intended to write, *A Concern For Weaving.*) (23)

CHAPTER 2

The Classic Moorman Exercise

WORKING THROUGH THE exercises Theo presents in her *Weaving as an Art Form* is still an excellent way to learn this technique. If this is the first Moorman book you own, you may start right here with our adaptation of Theo's exercises.

This chapter gives general advice on equipment and yarn and describes a classic Moorman exercise. It presupposes some basic knowledge about weaving. You need to be able to make a warp, dress the loom, and do plain weave. If you can handle these three activities, then you are ready for the Moorman technique. If you are already familiar with this weave, you may want to skip the exercise at the end of this chapter.

Equipment

A four-shaft jack loom that can raise one shaft while leaving three down is needed for this technique. The directions in this book are written for a jack, or rising shed, floor loom. A table loom in good working order is fine for learning the technique.

A second warp beam is not necessary to weave this structure. You may, however, have tension problems if you try to put a long warp on a single warp beam for the Theo Moorman technique. For warps up to two and a half yards in length, the tie-down warp and the ground warp can be wound together on single warp beam. A second warp beam to hold the tie-down warp is an advantage if you are planning warps three yards and longer. A second warp beam should also be used for the tie-down warp if you use several different weights of pattern weft in your design or if you plan unequal areas of design on the surface. Directions for warping two beams are included in chapter 6 and in the book and video *Warping on a Shoestring.*

A well-lighted weaving space is also necessary. When ground warps and tie-down warps are the same color, the fine tie-down warps can disappear against the ground. Black on black, although very striking to weave with, is most difficult to see. Because the tie-down yarns are very fine, it is easy to leave floats where you have

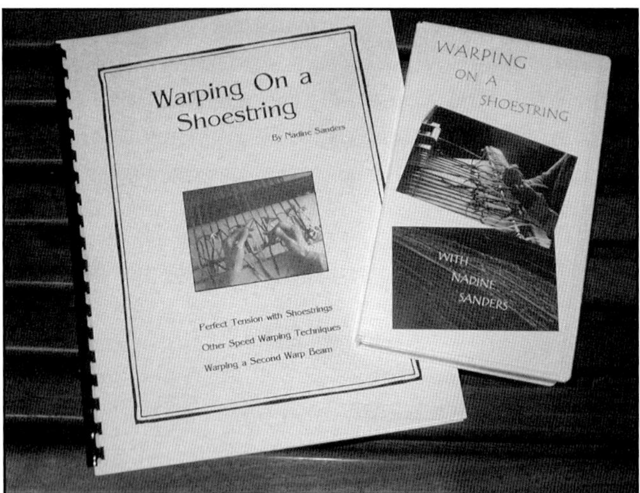

***Warping on a Shoestring* describes speed warping and using a second warp beam.**

Full spectrum lighting makes it easier to see the tie-down warps.

skipped over a tie-down warp or misjudged the entry point of the pattern weft shuttle. Some weavers use full spectrum florescent ceiling lights or lamps clipped directly to the loom. Others prefer natural light from a skylight or large window, combined with artificial lighting. If your eyesight is not perfect or your lighting is not optimal, choose tie-down yarns that contrast with the ground warp color or wind a tie-down warp with alternating colors: black, gray, black, gray.

Warp materials

Theo Moorman preferred a white ground warp with black tie-down warps. Our classic Moorman exercise uses 10/2 cotton for the ground warp and 20/2 cotton for the tie-down warp.

Warping and threading the loom

When using a single warp beam for a small project, the ground warp and the tie-down warp can be measured and wound onto the beam together. To wind two warps together, use two cones of yarns for the ground warp and one cone for the tie-down warp, and wind all as one.

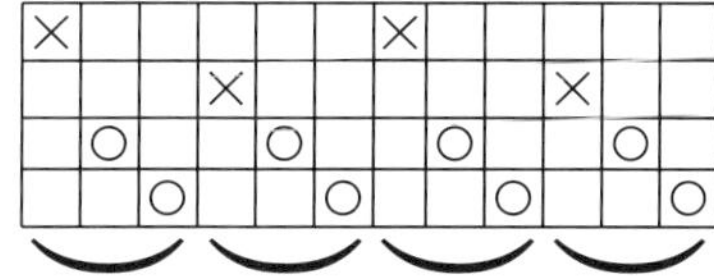

In this draft of the Moorman warping order, X represents a tie-down, and 0 represents a ground thread.

The instructions in this book are for warping the loom from back to front. I find it easier to keep the fine tie-down warps from tangling around the ground warp by threading *back to front*. Skilled front to back warpers can be successful, but I have had students in workshops who said afterwards, "Why didn't you *make* me warp back to front?" Experience is the best teacher! Try both methods, then decide.

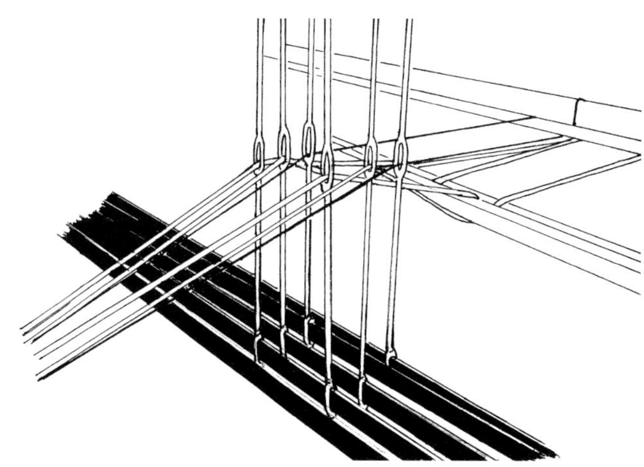

Threading by groups of six will help you keep track of where you are in the threading sequence.

Thread in groups of six:

a. ground warp onto shafts 1 and 2 and fine tie-down warp on shaft 3;

b. ground warp on shafts 1 and 2, then fine tie-down warp on shaft 4.

Repeat.

Since the pattern of threading is 1,2,3; 1,2,4—an error will quickly become apparent if you are out of sequence.

Sleying the reed

In classic Moorman threading, the threads are sleyed three to a dent in a twelve-dent reed.

Tying on

When warping from back to front:

After the warp has been sleyed, grasp a six-inch width of warp in your hands and raise the tie-down warps by pressing down on treadles 3 and 4. (If warping front to back, do this step after you have wound on the warp and are ready to tie onto the rod of the cloth beam.) Pay attention that the fine tie-down yarns do not slide out of the reed as you raise them. Lift the fine tie-down yarns above the heavier ground warp. Lifting the fine yarns allows them to tension separately. Check to see that the tie-down warps are all

Lift the tie-down yarns free of the ground warp before tying them onto the front beam. This trick will keep the warp yarns from sticking to each other.

threaded. Also check that none of the tie-down yarns is twisted around a ground warp. If so, this is the time to fix them. Pull tight each group of fine and heavy warp threads before you fasten them to the front cloth beam. I tie on and tension with shoestrings, a speed warping method Joyce learned when she was teaching weaving to high school students.

Tie-up

Tie up your treadles as follows: 1 and 3 together; 3 alone; 4 alone; 2 and 4 together. If you have a fifth and sixth treadle, they should be left unattached in the center. With this tie-up, each sequence can be completed on the side from which you throw the ground shuttle. Your left foot moves from treadle 3 to treadle 1-3 for the first sequence; your right foot moves from treadle 4 to treadle 2-4 to complete the second sequence. With this tie-up, you can go away from the loom in the middle of a sequence and come back to know exactly where you are by seeing where the shuttles are.

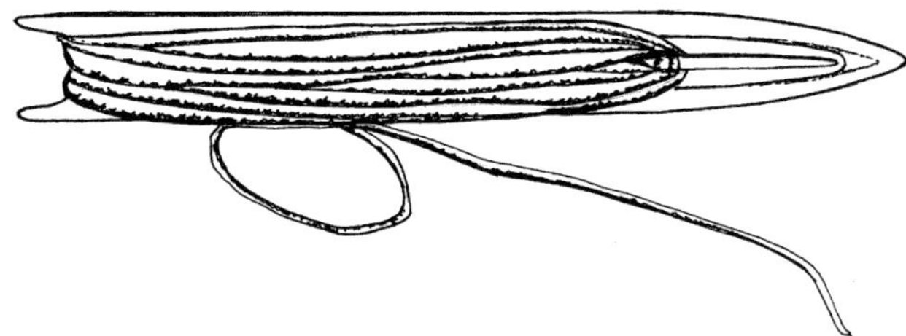

Netting shuttles are available from commercial fishing suppliers and from The Singing Weaver.

Shuttles

You can use a variety of shuttles for Theo Moorman weaving. Boat shuttles or end-feed shuttles are the best choice for the ground weft on a wide warp. Stick shuttles of varying lengths are useful on narrow warps.

A netting shuttle, originally used by fishers in making nets, is a useful tool. Try using netting shuttles instead of butterflies for small amounts of yarn. Four- and six-inch netting shuttles are appropriate for laying in pattern weft; the eight-inch size is useful for larger areas of pattern inlay, for thick yarns, or for ground weft on narrower weavings. Netting shuttles made of sturdy but flexible plastic are most useful. An additional benefit of using netting shuttles is that the white shuttle tip inserted under the fine tie-down threads makes the tie-downs easy to see.

To wind a netting shuttle

1. Grasp the shuttle in one hand. Hold the tail of the yarn against the middle of the shuttle with your thumb.
2. With the other hand, push down the shuttle tip on the front side of the shuttle and wrap the yarn around the thin narrow "tongue" of the shuttle.

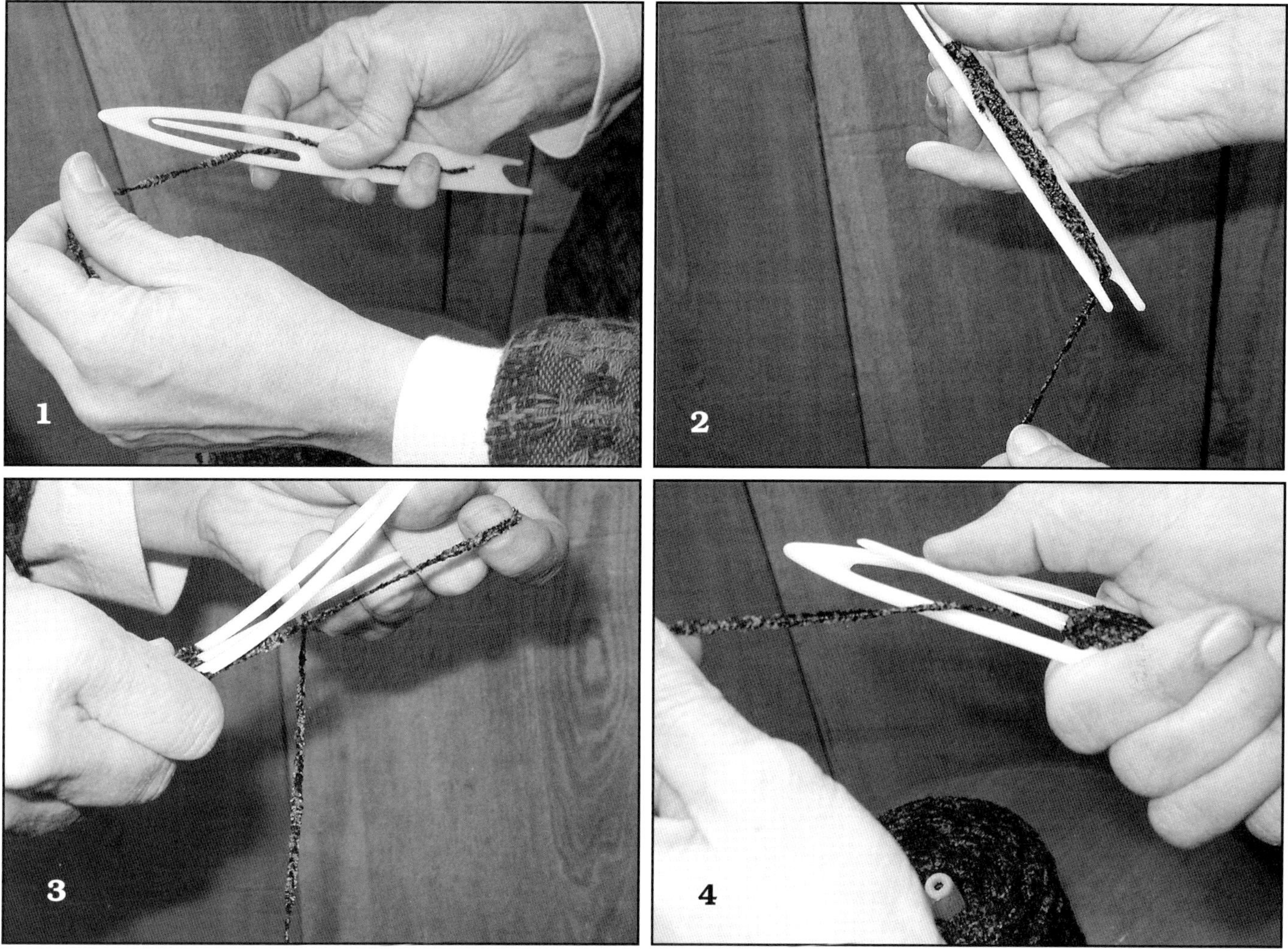

WINDING A NETTING SHUTTLE

1. Begin by holding the tail of the yarn against the middle of the shuttle with your thumb. 2. Alternate winding the yarn from front to back of the shuttle. 3. Push shuttle tip away from tongue with back of thumb. 4. Continue wrapping yarn on the shuttle, alternating from front to back.

3. Bring the yarn down to the bottom, two-pronged end of the shuttle and place it in the curved depression. Bring the yarn to the back side of the shuttle.
4. Push up on the shuttle tip from the back side of the shuttle and wrap the yarn around the narrow "tongue."
5. Bring the yarn down to the bottom of the shuttle (back side) and place it in the curved depression area at the bottom. Bring the yarn to the front side of the shuttle.
6. Continue wrapping yarn on the shuttle, alternating front to back side.

Beginning, splicing, enlarging, and finishing

Because this is a two-layer warp, there are special ways of starting and ending weft yarns.

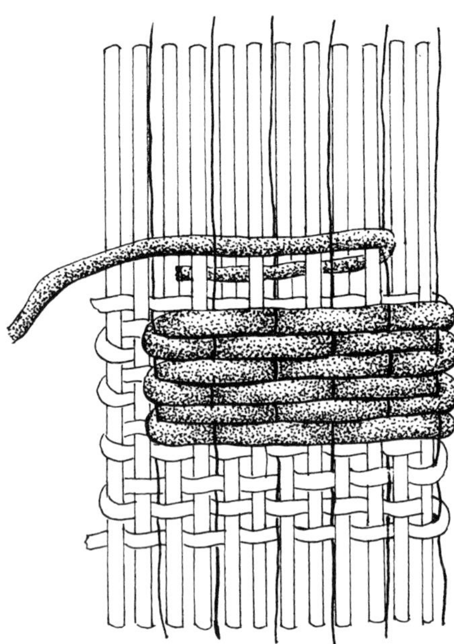

Begin a new pattern weft by burying the end in the ground shed.

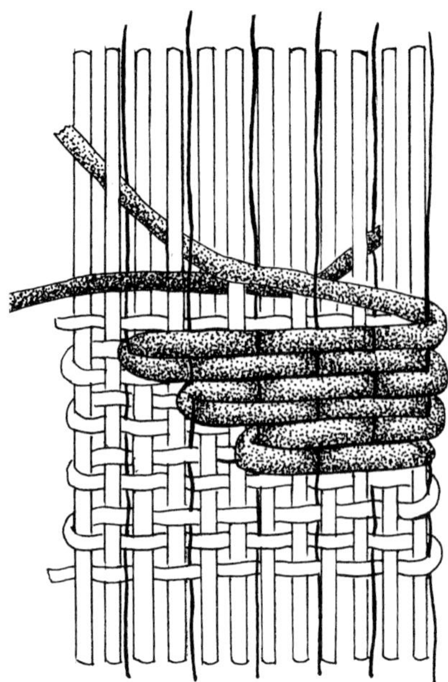

Splice pattern wefts by burying both old and new ends in the ground shed.

Beginning a pattern weft

Three inches of the tail of the pattern weft yarn is laid into the current ground shed, (1-3) or (2-4). Close the ground fabric shed and bring the pattern weft up between two tie-down threads. With the desired tie-down shaft (3 or 4) raised, place the pattern weft under the tie-down, close the shed, and beat. The end of the pattern weft will be buried in with the ground weft once it has been beaten into place. You need to bury the tail within a design area, or it will show in the ground fabric.

Splicing a pattern weft

To splice a pattern weft, lay the end of the new pattern weft in the ground shed overlapping the tail of the completed pattern weft. Bring the new pattern weft up between tie-down yarns. The splice is buried in the ground fabric. Weaving continues as above.

Starting at a point in a design area

Let a tail of three or four inches of pattern weft hang below the cloth. Bring the shuttle up through the ground fabric where the point will begin. Go around a tie-down warp, encircling it. Throw the ground warp. On the next row, pick up the tie-down thread used in the last sequence and encircle it again, building up the point. Throw the ground warp. On the third shed move to the next tie-down and go under it. Keep increasing the size of the shape by working out from the point. Narrow lines or areas can also be developed in this way; broadening them a little at a time will create a slender design element, such as a crescent moon or a shaft of light.

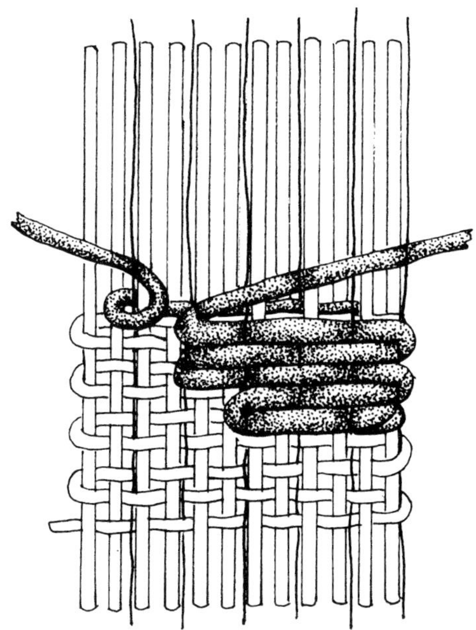

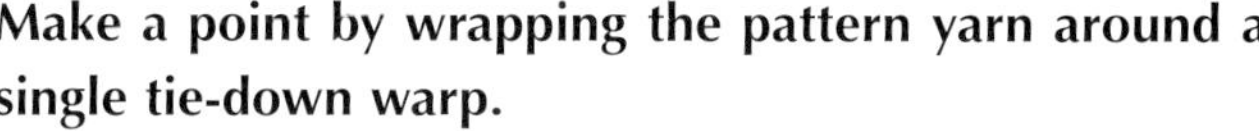

Make a point by wrapping the pattern yarn around a single tie-down warp.

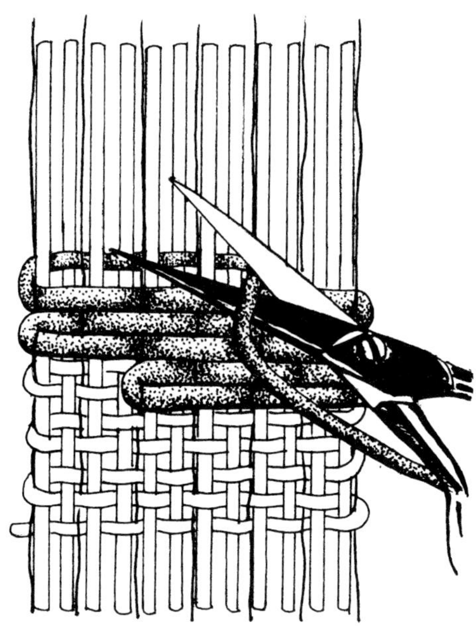

To end a pattern weft, bury the end in the ground shed.

Ending with a point

To end with a point, encircle a tie-down warp. Throw the ground warp. On the next row, pick up the tie-down warp from the previous shed and encircle it again. The thickness of the yarn will determine the number of consecutive rows in which you will need to encircle the same tie-down to create a sharp point. Cut off the pattern inlay yarn leaving a three- or four-inch tail. With a tapestry needle, bury three-quarters of an inch of the tail end in the design area on the surface of the weaving. Cut off the excess thread.

Ending a pattern weft

When cutting off a pattern weft at the conclusion of a design area, only a half-inch of the tail needs to be laid back under the design area in the current ground shed. Beat it into place. Throw the next ground weft, and beat it. This sequence locks the pattern thread into place. Any design area that is at least one-half inch wide or more can be started or ended this way; for narrower areas use the method described above for ending a point.

Weaving Moorman

When you are ready to begin, weave two inches of plain weave (1-3, 2-4) for a hem. The weaving sequence is detailed on the draft on page 10.

If you have tied up your loom as suggested at the beginning of this chapter, both shuttles will start from the side where you are treadling. You can find your place easily when you have been away from your weaving.

Some weavers, following Theo Moorman's instruction, place the ground weft first and follow it with the pattern weft. If this order seems more natural for you, by all means use it. The weaving order, whether pattern-ground or ground-pattern, makes no difference, so long as it is consistent.

On the next two pages you will find a draft for a classic Moorman exercise. The exercise uses simple shapes to demonstrate the techniques described in this unit.

The Classic Moorman Exercise

Ends per inch: 36

Finished piece: 8″ x 14″

Warp: 288 ends wound together by threes
24 ground warps, 10/2 light color cotton = O
12 tie-down warp, 20/2 dark color cotton = X
36 ends per inch

Reed: 12-dent reed, three ends per dent

Warping: For a short warp of one to two and one-half yards, ground warp and tie-down warp may be rolled on together. Spread the ground warp and the tie-down warp and fasten them to the back beam. Wind on. Then proceed to thread all the yarns through the heddles and the reed. When you are ready to weave, it is good to check the threading and tension of both warp yarns. The tension of the ground warp and the tie-down warp should be the same.

*The half-moon shapes underneath the threading chart indicate ends sleyed in the same dent in the reed.

Weaving:
When you are ready to begin, weave two inches of plain weave (1-3), (2-4) for a hem.
Bury the tail of the pattern inlay weft in the current ground shed.

Sequence A, Row One

Step 1. With shaft 3 raised, lay the pattern weft yarn under the tie-down warp to the edge of the desired design area. Close the shed.

Step 2. Raise shafts 1 and 3. Throw the ground weft shuttle across the shed, close the shed, and beat both wefts into place.

Sequence B, Row Two

Step 3. Raise shaft 4. Lay the pattern weft under the tie-down warp to fill in the next row of the design area. Close the shed.

Step 4. Raise shafts 2 and 4. Throw the ground weft shuttle across the open shed, close shed, and beat both wefts into place.

Repeat steps 1 through 4.

Note: The schematic tie-up shown on this page is different from that described in words on page 6. The tie-up on this page has the tabby sheds side by side for ease in showing how the weave works. The tie-up described on page 6 puts the tabby treadles on the sides of the tie-up, with the pattern treadles between them. Both tie-ups produce the same result.

This design for a wall hanging reviews the exercises that Theo Moorman suggests in her book, *Weaving as an Art Form.* If you are not accustomed to weaving with two weft shuttles, you may want to start with the sample on this page. The directions are to be read **from the bottom to the top,** as they would be woven. Each instruction corresponds to the section of the sample directly to its right.

F. Free-form shapes demonstrate another effect that is possible with this weave.

E. Stepping up the tie-down yarns one or two at a time will show how diagonal shapes are created. Add some textured yarn while you are weaving to see the effect of using two shuttles in the same shed.

D. One of the advantages of this weave is the facility to create curved forms. Use a medium weight pattern weft and concentrate on keeping the curves very smooth.

C. Add a third block to learn how to handle several shuttles at once.

B. Then add a second shuttle to create a second block.

A. Begin with an inch or so of a single block of pattern weft.

Chapter 3

Variation: A Firm Opaque Fabric

Moorman is a variation of plain weave. If you consider how many different weights and qualities of plain weave you can weave depending on the sett and the materials you choose, you will begin to appreciate the variations that are possible. Once you understand how this structure works, you can create your own sett and choose appropriate materials for the type of fabric you desire. From very dense to transparent, as long as you use the ratio of one tie-down to two ground warps, the structure will be sound.

Both the sett and the yarns play an important role in creating a firm, opaque fabric. When Joyce began weaving in the Theo Moorman technique, she was looking for a firm fabric that would hang well and accommodate large design elements. She had been using some vibrant rayon yarns, comparable to Harrisville's Shetland wool, and wanted to continue using those yarns. Adapting this new technique required some experimentation.

She experimented with metallic tie-downs as fine as 20/2 cotton and found that fine gimp held up very well in combination with the heavy ground warp yarns. The weight of the fabric meant that it was possible to inlay a design in just part of the ground and still have good tension. (Usually one would balance the design areas not only to have a pleasing design, but also to keep the tension between the tie-down warp and the ground warp compatible.) Joyce also reduced the thirty-six ends per inch of the classical method to twenty-four ends per inch—sixteen ground warps and eight tie-downs. (Joyce's opaque draft is at the end of this chapter.)

This firm fabric hung well with no lining. This consideration was important in her commission work for churches because it eliminated the time-consuming and expensive step of lining. Her liturgical stoles won acceptance because they stayed in place, were not too heavy, and continued to hang well over a period of years. This opaque, firm fabric became even more important when she began to weave wall hangings up to seventeen feet long. These needed to hang well and rest flat against the wall.

Materials: Ground warp

Two-ply Harrisville Shetland wool, 5/2 perle cotton from DMC, or wool crepe yarns work well as ground warp for heavier, opaque fabric. In Joyce's early liturgical work, she combined one strand of wool and one strand of rayon so two threads functioned as one ground warp. She threaded these together as one in the heddles. A good combination of materials readily available today is one strand of Harrisville's two-ply Shetland wool with one strand of 5/2 perle cotton by DMC or one strand of wool crepe.

Tie-down warp

The tie-down warp is 20/2 cotton or the equivalent in silk or rayon. I prefer UKI perle cotton primarily because it comes in more than one hundred forty colors.

Although silk would not be as common for tie-down warp in a firm opaque fabric as it would be in clothing fabric, it would work well in both applications. Tie-down warp could be 30/2 or 60/2 Bombyx silk, 2-ply reeled Bombyx, 60/4 silk/cotton, or 60/4 silk/ramie. As Tencel becomes more available in the United States, a 20/2 equivalent of this fiber is also an option.

For traditional pieces, a tie-down warp in the same color as the ground warp is used. Thus in areas where there is no pattern inlay, the tie-down warp disappears against the ground. I often use two or more related colors of tie-down yarns when making the warp—peach and beige, black and gray, gold and yellow. At first the reason was so students could more easily see the tie-down warp against the ground warp when threading and inlaying. But I also like the subtle variation it gives to the appearance of the fabric.

For many of her earlier liturgical weavings, Joyce used a metallic tie-down that is no longer available. She liked the vibrancy it gave when viewed from a distance. Currently in the United States, it is difficult to find a metallic thread or yarn that will work as tie-down warp. The metallic yarn needs to have three characteristics:

a. *strong*—needs to have a polyester or cotton core;
b. *pliable*—metallic must be wound around the core; often this winding makes the metallic yarn too stiff;
c. *thin*—there are a number of metallics for the embroidery industry that are thin enough but don't meet the first two characteristics. There are also some metallics for weavers that are strong and pliable, but too thick for tie-down warp. They will detract from the design and make the piece look gaudy.

Sleying variation

Two ground warps and the tie-down on shaft 4 are sleyed together in one dent. Then the tie-down warp on shaft 3 is sleyed by itself in a dent. Then two ground warps are sleyed together in a dent. The sequence repeats. Students often ask about the unusual sleying in the opaque draft. Joyce adopted this sleying for several reasons. The most important reason was that this sleying order would create a pattern of the tie-down warps in the reed. The tie-down warp on shaft 3 is always sleyed singly. Thanks to this pattern, it is easy to catch sleying errors. Another test of this threading is to lift the tie-down warps above the ground warps before tying on. They should rise in pairs. When Joyce reduced the number of ends per inch to twenty-four to accommodate the heavy warp, she found that this sleying order also prevented the heavy warp yarns from sticking in the reed.

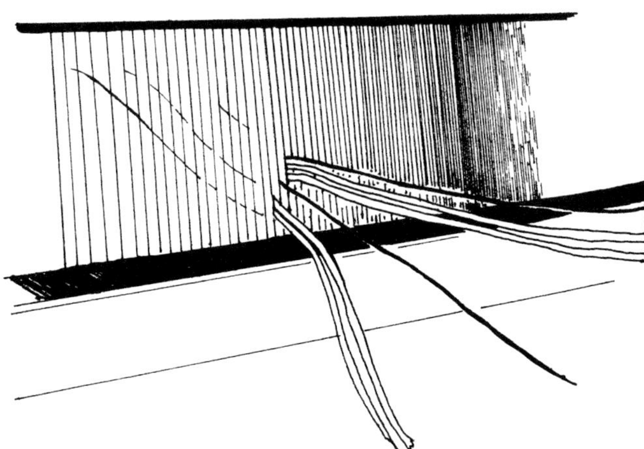

In a twelve-dent reed, sley three ends—two ground warps and one tie-down—together, then a single tie-down alone, and then two ground warps together.

Weft yarns

Experimentation is one of the joys of weaving with the Moorman technique; having two wefts doubles the field for experimentation. When I teach the technique, students always comment on how surprised they are by the wide variety of weft yarns Moorman warps will accommodate. For a firm opaque fabric, the ground weft yarn should be nearly the same size as the ground warp yarn. For a traditional look, choose weft yarns that are the same color as the warp yarns. With the Harrisville Shetland 2-ply and 5/2 cotton combination, a good choice for weft is one strand of Harrisville's 2-ply wool. Weaving several rows of plain weave (1-3; 2-4) will let you test the desired amount of beating necessary to achieve a balanced weave.

Pattern weft

For pattern wefts, there is even more variety. The pattern inlay yarns lie on the surface of the ground fabric and really show. So the pattern weft is the place to use rich, luxurious, precious yarns! You may want to make a very plain ground fabric just to let the inlay yarns zing!

Pattern inlay effects

The kind of materials you choose depends on the pattern inlay effect you choose: transparent, opaque, or saturated.

Transparent effect means that the pattern inlay yarn is significantly thinner than the ground weft. When inlaying designs, you will still be able to see the ground behind the design area.

Opaque effect means that the pattern inlay weft is the same size or slightly larger than the ground weft. Designs will appear solid and no ground will show through.

Saturated effect is achieved by using very thick pattern inlay yarns, much thicker than the ground weft. The saturated effect gives you a very textured surface and draws attention to itself. This effect may cause the ground fabric to distort because of the disparity between the ground and pattern weft sizes. Here are several ways to overcome this distortion:

1. Inlay the thick pattern weft, then weave two rows of ground.
2. Balance the design areas that use the saturated effect.
3. Inlay extra shots of ground weft on either side of the design area where you are using the saturated effect.

Rhythm and Effect Exercise: Transparent, Opaque, and Saturated Effects

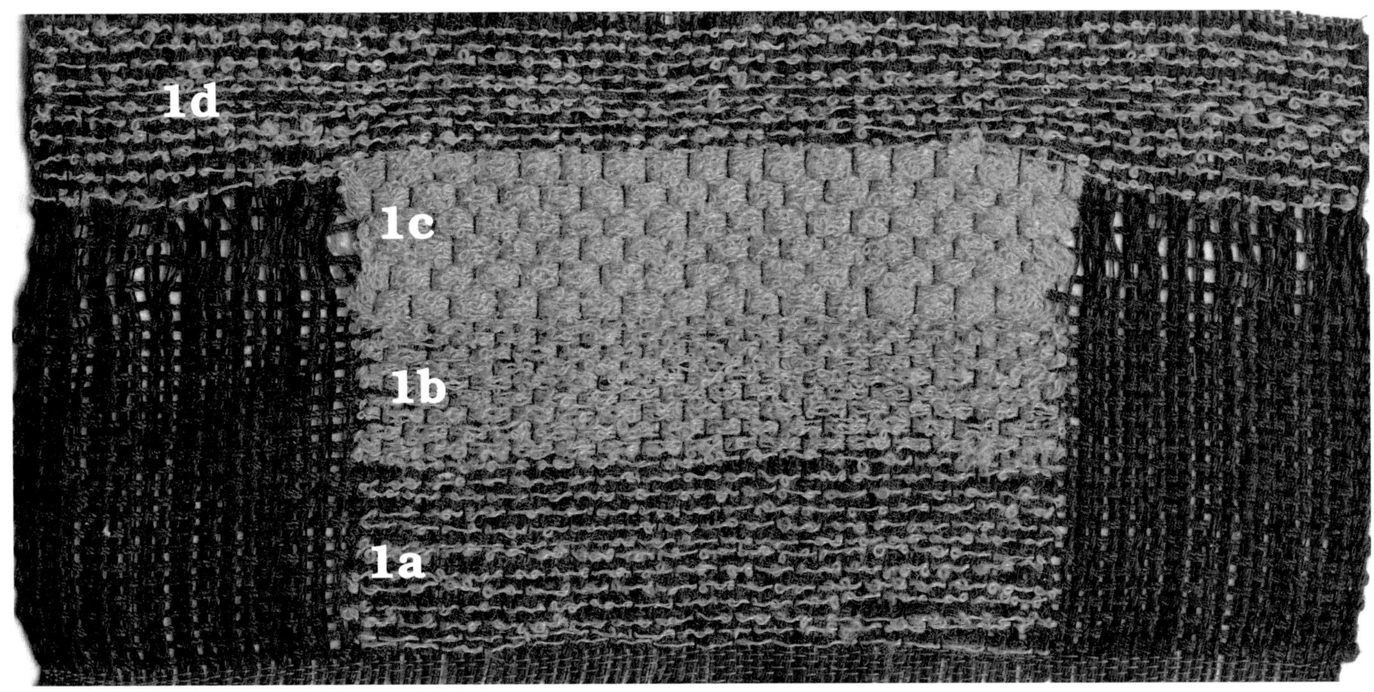

Use the same ground weft for 1a, 1b, 1c and 1d.

1a. Transparent Effect

Weave a 2″ x 6″ rectangle with a single or doubled pattern inlay yarn.

You should be able to see the ground weft through the pattern inlay area. Sewing thread or 20/2 cotton might be a good choice for pattern inlay.

1b. Opaque Effect

Weave a 2″ x 6″ rectangle with 2, 3, or 4 strands of pattern weft.

The pattern inlay yarn should be equal in thickness or slightly thicker than the ground weft.

1c. Saturated Effect

Weave a 2″ x 6″ rectangle with a very thick pattern weft, four to eight strands.

Pattern inlay yarn should be as thick as a pencil.

After weaving 1c, notice how the ground fabric spreads apart when inlaying such a thick pattern weft.

1d. Choose the effect you like best: transparent, opaque or saturated

Inlay the pattern weft from edge to edge, for two inches, totally covering the ground weft. This is a quick way to fix the distorted ground created when weaving 1c. Don't forget to keep throwing the ground weft in addition to the pattern inlay weft.

I use all kinds of pattern inlay yarns. But the yarns I keep coming back to are silks and rayons because I like their sheen and vibrancy. I often use commercially dyed yarns for the warp and ground weft, but hand-dyed yarns for pattern inlay.

Some of the best novelty yarns available today are knitting yarns. Trendsetter Yarns is a clearing house of over one hundred fifty different brands of novelty yarns. They are a good place to start in your search. For further information, see *Knitting with Novelty Yarns* by Laura Militzer Bryant and Barry Klien.

Combinations of color and texture should be considered. Blending two or three different yarns can add depth and luminosity to the pattern inlay areas. Theo Moorman often spoke of the joy and importance of dyeing and blending colors.

> *"I recently studied closely the colours of an abalone shell that I brought back from New Zealand. In my recent weaving I had just achieved a subtle luminosity in the texture by a system of blending fine strands of shiny rayon with linen and an extremely fine metallic thread. The shell and the new texture 'married' and triggered off a whole series of new works. I was not attempting to simulate shells but to use something of the special quality of colour allied to luminosity that I saw."* (36, *Theo Moorman*, Diaper)

Variegated yarns can add interest to your pattern inlay design, but if the "repeat" length of the variegated yarn is similar to the width of the inlay design, unwanted stripes can result.

Mohair and other fuzzy yarns work very well for pattern inlay. More discussion of them can be found in chapter 9, Moorman Clothing.

Handspun yarn won't be lost in the background when used as pattern inlay. Handspun singles and novelty yarn work particularly well. For more discussion on using handspun see chapter 11, Gateways.

Fabric strips cut from quilting or clothing fabrics should not be overlooked. For suggestions on how to use fabric see chapter 8, Painting With Fabric Strips and chapter 11, Gateways.

Beyond yarns, an endless array of unusual materials can be used as pattern weft. Horsehair, ribbon, beads, feathers, paper, pine needles, and wheat are just a few of the possibilities. The Gateways chapter contains more information about unusual wefts.

Weaving techniques for pattern inlay weft

In teaching ways to translate graphic designs to fabric, the following terms describe methods of layering and texturing the surface design: *interrupt, weave-under* and *crossover.*

Interrupt: Large areas of a second color are placed on the background pattern inlay.

Detail, Advent altar hanging, Atonement Lutheran Church, St. Cloud, MN

Interrupt: larger shapes on a background pattern. Five shuttles were used to create this inlay design. From left to right: shuttle 1, blue; shuttle 2, white; shuttle 3, blue; shuttle 4, white; shuttle 5, blue. JH

When inlaying large areas of color in a design, you may find that you cannot carry one shuttle across the whole design; you need to interrupt a continuous block of color to weave around an interrupting shape. You can accomplish this weaving smoothly by using two or more shuttles of the main pattern weft.

1. Weave across the pattern until you come to the interrupting shape.

2. Bring the first pattern weft to the surface.
3. Inlay the interrupting shape with a second shuttle of a different colored yarn; weave to the end of this shape; bring this shuttle to the surface.
4. Using a third shuttle wound with the main pattern weft, weave the rest of the way across the design area.
5. Beat all.
6. Switch to the ground shed, throw the ground weft and beat.

Weave-under: a small shape is placed in the middle of a field of another color.

Generally weave-under is useful only for areas smaller than two or three inches across. If you will be creating a larger spot of color, then you should use the interrupt technique so as not to build up too much extra bulk in the design area. Weave-under is nonetheless a more economical use of time and shuttles than weaving in and around these shapes with many small shuttles. Weave-under causes the small shape to stand out and add texture to the work.

1. Wind two netting shuttles: one with the main colored pattern weft and a second with a different colored pattern weft.
2. Raise shaft 3 or 4 and put the main pattern weft through the shed until you come to the edge of the small shape.
3. Change to the appropriate ground shed (1-3) or (2-4)) and tunnel through the ground shed with the main pattern weft shuttle until you come to the other edge of the small shape. Change back to the pattern shed (shaft 3 or 4) and inlay the rest of the design area with the main pattern inlay shuttle.
4. With the pattern shed still raised, weave the small area with the second pattern weft.
5. Beat both pattern wefts.
6. Open the ground shed and throw the ground weft; beat.

The main pattern weft has traveled through the ground shed behind the small design area. Weave-under can not be used if there is not a second color of pattern inlay to cover up the area where the main pattern inlay yarn is traveling through the ground.

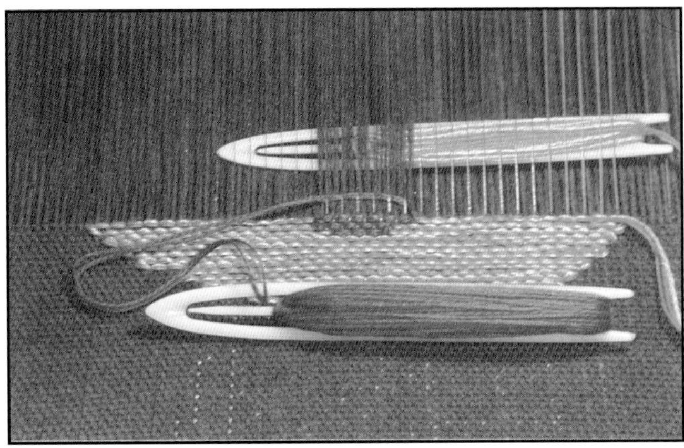

WEAVE-UNDER. The background yarn goes under the tie-down warp until it comes to the small shape. Then it tunnels through the ground warp and comes back into the pattern shed on other side of the small shape.

Crossover: Two pattern weft shuttles in the same shed cross over each other.

This technique uses two pattern shuttles in the same shed. This can be used to make the pattern area more dense, to create a shadow, or to give designs a layered appearance. Crossover can involve two shuttles with the same color yarn of the same or different thickness; two shuttles with two different colors of yarn of the same or different thickness; or three or more shuttles if a number of design motifs are coming together in one area. One pattern inlay shuttle carries a color one direction while another shuttle goes the opposite direction. They cross over each other in either shed 3 or shed 4. When laying in two colors, take care always to weave the colors in the same order so as not to develop a striped effect. Too many crossovers may create tension problems because you are building up an area of the design with several thicknesses of inlay yarn. Crossovers need to be kept to a minimum or distributed evenly throughout the design.

DETAIL, ALTAR HANGING CHRIST LUTHERAN CHURCH, EAST NORTHPORT, LONG ISLAND, NY
An example of the crossover technique: although the fish appears to be behind the waves, the shapes were all woven at the same time. JH

Turn-arounds

It is not necessary to have all the shuttles going the same direction in this technique; sometimes it is better to have shuttles going opposite directions on curves and diagonal lines. Having shuttles go in opposite directions helps define the edges of curves more accurately.

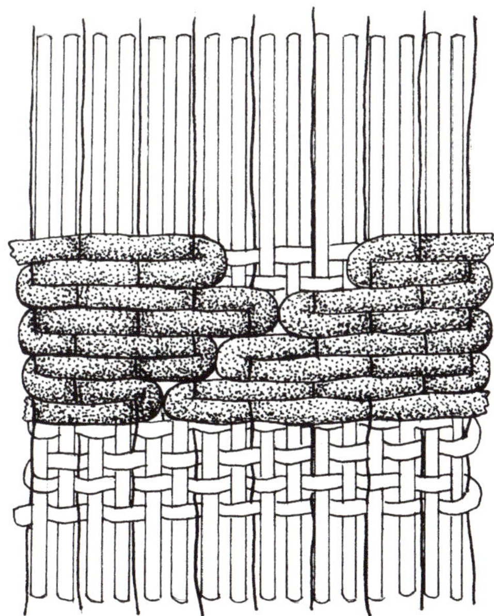

A turn-around should wrap neatly around a tie-down thread.

There is no need to join the different pattern inlay yarns when they meet at design edges as you would in true tapestry, because the pattern inlay yarn is sitting on a solid ground. The *turn-arounds* define the edge of the shapes and add texture. I want my weavings to look like fiber, not some other medium; I use the distinct line that the turn-arounds make to accentuate the design. A variation some weavers have used is to eliminate the turn-arounds on the surface. They drop the pattern inlay shuttle to the backside of the weaving before throwing the ground weft. This puts the turn-arounds on the backside and gives the surface of the weaving a flat, photographic quality.

Weaving Moorman

The Theo Moorman technique is not a complicated weave. It requires care in selecting warp and weft materials and in dressing the loom. It also requires some practice to produce curves and other shapes accurately and effectively. However, the actual weaving is quite simple and quickly produces a striking fabric. The effectiveness of the completed fabric depends on the harmony between the design and the weave structure. To that interrelationship we turn in the next chapters.

A small project using the draft for a firm, opaque fabric is detailed on the next pages.

You may want to make the project warp longer to practice inlaying circles, triangles, and curves before attempting the project.

Exercise: Painting Shapes with the Pattern Inlay Yarn

The Moorman structure allows you to break out of the grid and create shapes with inlay yarns. Since these shapes are on the surface of the ground and held in place by tie-down warps, there is no need to stick to squares or rectangles. This exercise will help you become free by using the pattern inlays shuttles like paintbrushes or crayons. Your eye and your hand will discover how to translate shapes from your head to the woven cloth.

For this exercise, large shapes are much easier to weave than small delicate shapes.

Choose a pattern inlay yarn and either the transparent or opaque inlay effect.

You can make the shapes one at a time, or you can start the circle and, halfway through, begin to use a second shuttle to start the triangle on the other side of the warp. Similarly you can initiate the curve while you are still weaving the triangle.

Circle

Picture a circle in your head. Aim for a circle at least as large as the drawing on this page. The length of the base of your circle will determine how big your circle will be.

I suggest starting with the circle, because some students find that once they start their circle it metamorphoses into a triangle! Use your eye and the shuttle to paint the circle. You will learn as you weave. Don't cheat and place a drawing of a circle underneath your warp or draw on the ground warp yarns.

Allow your circle to become whatever circular shape it may. An egg, a flying saucer, a Christmas ornament are all common results for first-time Theo Moorman weavers.

Here are a few hints:

Students have been known to try the circle up to three times. You will perfect it by the third time.

Try starting with fat or hairy inlay yarns. You don't have to be as exact about the circle edges and the design will still look circular.

On the other hand, using the transparent inlay effect where the pattern inlay yarn is much finer than the ground weft will really force you to be exact in your turn-around increments.

Pulling the edges of the pattern inlay tightly against the edge tie-down warp yarn when you turn around will give the circle a flatter look. Leaving a looser loop at the edge tie-down warp yarn when you turn around will give the circle volume. Does eyeballing the circle give you fits? Chapter 6 gives instructions for making and using a cartoon.

Triangle

Choose a different pattern inlay yarn and either the transparent or opaque inlay effect. Remember, larger shapes are much easier to create than small delicate shapes.

Picture a triangle in your head. Any type of triangle is fine but an equilateral triangle is easier. Aim for a triangle at least as large as the drawing on this page.

Start with the base of the triangle. A general rule is to step in every other row on alternating edges with the pattern inlay shuttle.

When you are within several rows of the point, determine which tie-down warp yarn will become the top of point. When you reach the point stage, encircle the tie-down warp with the pattern inlay yarn, throw the ground and beat. In the next row, pick up the same tie-down warp, encircle it with pattern yarn, throw the ground, and beat. In the third row, encircle the tie-down yarn, throw the ground, and beat. Usually two or three rows of encircling the point are required to achieve a point. Cut off the pattern inlay yarn, leaving a four-inch tail. With a tapestry needle, needle-weave the tail into the surface of the triangle shape. You can further refine the point by pulling the tail tight to minimize the point, or leave the tail rather loose to add a vertical stroke to a blunt point.

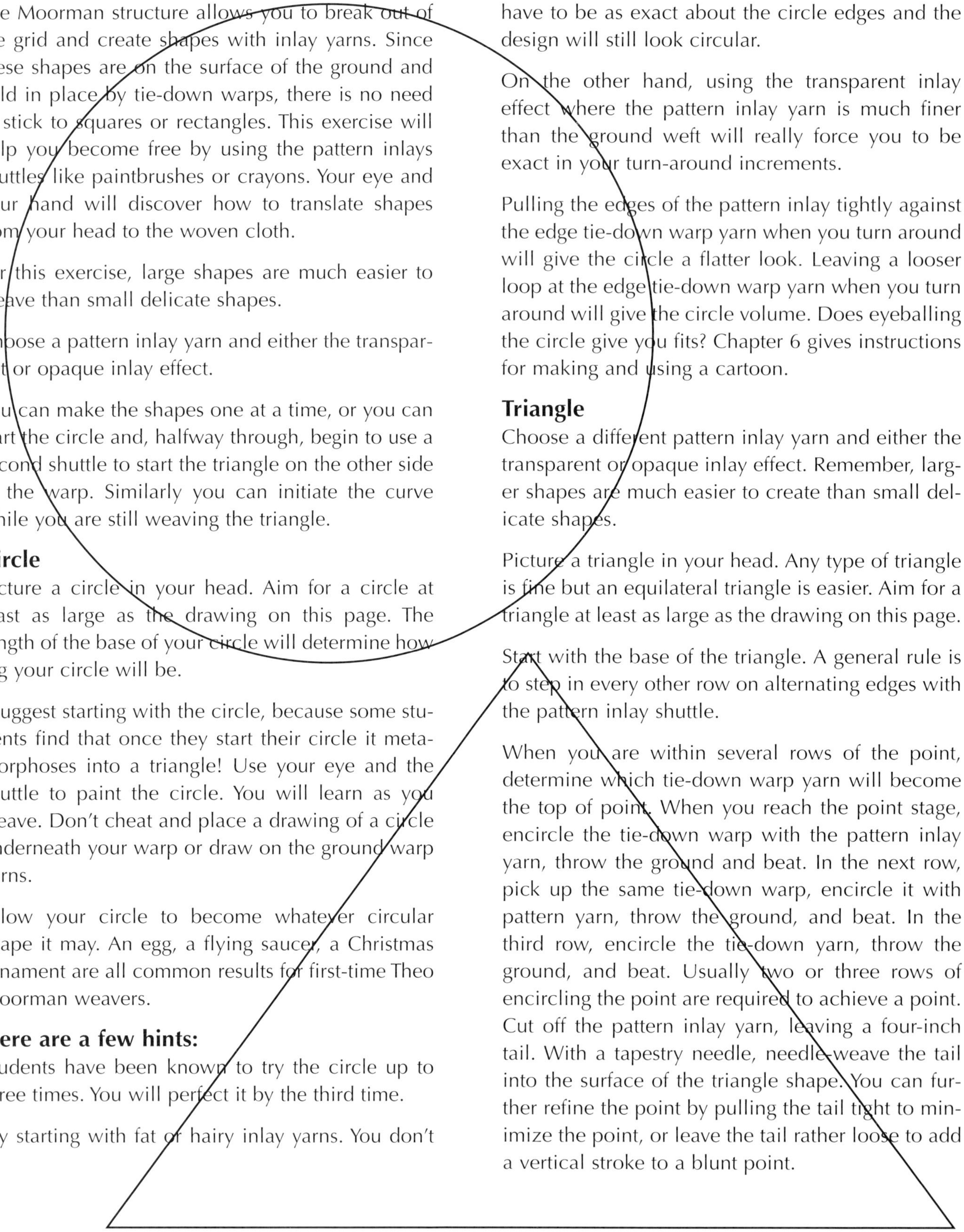

Curve
Choose a different pattern inlay yarn and either the transparent or opaque inlay effect.

Picture a curved shape in your head. A curve that accelerates is a good challenge. The curve that changes widths is also fun to weave. Think about a crescent moon, a meandering stream, or the tail of a comet.

Curve Hints:
Some curves may require that you use two shuttles in different areas of the same row.
Curves that are more vertical than horizontal are easier to weave.
If weaving these curves thrills you, you have found the technique to match your free style!
If this shape throws you a curve, you will really appreciate the cartoon in chapter 6.

Opaque Draft: A firm fabric for wall hangings, pillows, table runners, placemats

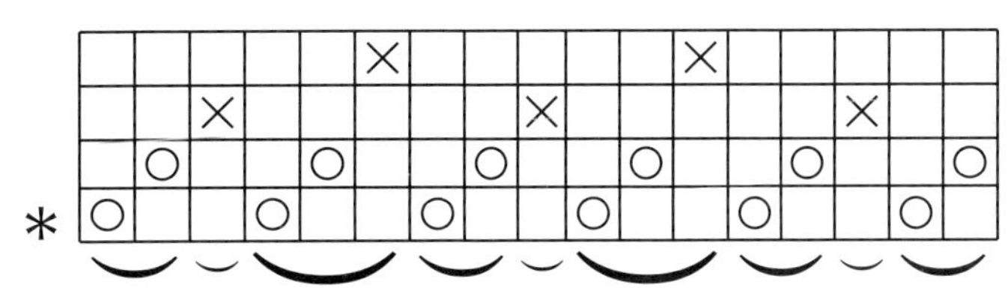

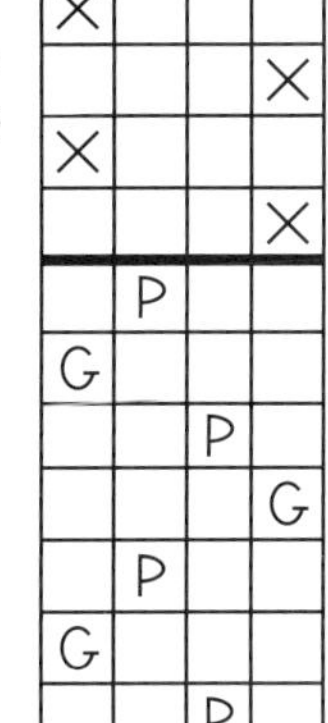

Ends per inch: 24

Ground: 16 ends, heavier yarn
Tie-Down: 8 ends, thin yarn

Warp:
Two ends 2-ply Shetland wool or equivalent wound together as one = O
One end 20/2 cotton = X

Reed: 12 dent, sleying order as follows:
3 ends—1,2,4 (two Os and one X)
1 end—3 (one X alone)
2 ends—1,2 (two Os)
Repeat

*The half-moon shapes underneath the threading chart show ends sleyed through one dent in the reed.

Weft: G=ground weft in same weight as ground warp or slightly finer
P=pattern weft in various weights and textures

Note: In this project as in all other instructions in this book, the right hand side of the warp is determined by the position of the weaver sitting at the loom. That is, the right side of the warp is at your right hand when you are facing the front beam of the loom.

Project continues on next page

Sampler Exploring Crossover, Interrupt, and Weave-under

This project is meant to be woven freehand without a cartoon. Do not be discouraged if you are not totally satisfied with the curves and shapes that come from this attempt. You are learning to use numerous pattern inlay shuttles at the same time. These directions are written to be read from the **bottom to the top**, as you weave this project.

6. Finishing: Needle-weave any pattern inlay yarns you forgot to bury in the ground shed. Steam press the weaving from the backside, and fuse a hem in the top and bottom of this weaving.

5. Weave-under is a useful technique for small shapes in the middle of a main background pattern inlay. It is more efficient than using many small shuttles of yarn.

4. Blocks of color next to each other require several shuttles. You are now covering up the entire ground with pattern inlay. Pull the pattern inlay yarns taut at the edge of the design for some shapes; for other shapes, leave the turn-arounds loose and bumpy.

3. Use two different color tones so you can see why it is necessary to keep the pattern weft shuttles in the same sequence as you weave the crossover. If you do not keep the shuttles in the same weaving order, you will have stripes rather than blended colors.

2. Overlap blocks and begin another color in a curved design area. Curved areas are developed by gradually stepping out the turn-arounds.

1. This sampler begins with overlapping blocks of pattern weft of the same color.

Chapter 4

Design-Weave Synthesis: Creating a Design on Paper

"The beginning is the most important part of the work."—Plato

Weavers designing in the Theo Moorman technique have great freedom. Instead of letting the loom control the design, the weaver controls the design. Curved shapes may be combined with rectangles; free-form shapes can be overlapped or used as isolated objects on the background. A single motif can be placed on the ground fabric or the entire ground can be covered with pattern inlay. While some weavers find this freedom exhilarating, many find it frightening because they have little or no design information to follow.

For the Theo Moorman technique, weavers must create their own designs. The purpose of this chapter is to facilitate this design process.

In the late twentieth century, many books arrived on the scene to help people discover and develop their creativity. New books arrive yearly. One of these books might be your starting place if you are new to the idea of creating your own designs. Besides working through these books on your own, many arts communities offer guided classes based on these books.

Books I would highly recommend are:

The New Drawing on the Right Side of the Brain by Betty Edwards

The Artist's Way: A Spiritual Path to Higher Creativity by Julia Cameron

Writing Down the Bones: Freeing the Writer Within by Natalie Goldberg, Judith Guest.

Time to begin: Designing worksheet

The list of questions on page 22 will help you define the design process for yourself. Write down your answers. In the future you may want to review these questions when you get stuck on a project, as you advance your skill with projects and classes, or as life experiences bring changes. You might find a common thread of interest that transcends the years or you may have totally different interests today from what you had ten years ago.

What is design?

When I ask weavers in my workshops to define "design," I get many different answers:

Design is taking abstract ideas and making them concrete.

Design is choosing colors and yarns.

Design is arranging objects in a space.

Design is working within limitations of size, color, budget, and still creating something unique.

Design is organizing thoughts or physical things into a pleasing composition.

Whether or not you believe it at this point, we are all designers already. We have arranged our weaving studios, our kitchens, our bedrooms to be useful living and working spaces. What you may not be pleased with is your organization of these spaces!

Designing is improved by the doing of it. Your design abilities will grow as you mature with this weave structure. Joyce has worked with the Moorman weave for thirty years, and still finds more and more ways to use it. She describes working with this weave as a design-weave synthesis. "I think of translating my drawings from paper to cloth as a process of integrating the design with the weave and the weave with the design. By blending the elements of design into the structure of the Moorman weave, it is possible to create weavings that can be no other way."

Within the framework of the design-weave synthesis, however, the process of designing is still highly individualized. Many adults have emerged from school frustrated by their inability to draw or build a composition of shapes.

Designing Worksheet: Time to Begin Questions

What am I interested in?
What do I collect? What do I throw away/recycle?
What inspires me in nature?
What magazines do I look at?
Who are my favorite artists/designers?
What books inspire me? What places inspire me?
How do the weather/seasons affect my creativity?
What are my excuses for not designing my own work?
Do I work best with a deadline or without a deadline?
What is my relationship to other creative arts? Music, dance, drama, video/movies, painting, sculpture, photography, mixed media, woodworking, clay, ceramics, metal, writing, other fiber arts?
How do I usually record/keep track of my ideas?
Do I like to draw? If I don't like to draw, why not?
My successful designs work because....
My unsuccessful designs don't work because...
How do I start the design process?
What are my favorite designing tools? Do I like to use technology in the design process (computer, camera, scanner, copy machine) or work low-tech?
What time of day am I most creative?
Where do I do my design work?
I have always wanted to design...
I like color because...
I don't like color because...

Am I inspired by my ethnic heritage or the ethnic cultures surrounding me?
Do I have a design file, box, drawer, envelopes to keep clippings?
What non-weaving friend can I discuss my designs with?
Which weaving friends can I discuss my designs with?

Some weavers have never had an opportunity to learn about art. Today the opportunities to learn at any age are endless.

Most community colleges offer basic design, art history, drawing, painting, graphics, and photography classes. If time or location is a restraint, many educational institutions have classes available via the internet. Many seniors enjoy Elderhostel classes that take place in locations throughout the world. Libraries increasingly have educational and instructional videos, DVDs, and CD-ROMs in their lending collections.

Designing with the aid of computers, scanners, digital imagery, and design software opens up endless paths to designing. This book focuses on designing with less technological tools. For information on technology-driven design see Resources for Ingrid Boesel and Sharon Marcus. These two weavers take different approaches to computer-aided design.

No matter how you initiate the design process, here are some basic concepts to keep in mind.

Spending more time in the design phase will increase the likelihood that you will produce a weaving that sings! Most often unsuccessful weavings fall short in the design phase.

Designing to scale is a good way to begin. If a

A photograph from an old National Geographic magazine was the inspiration for the curved design in the woven sample. JH

design is good in a small form, it has the potential to be a good design when woven at full-scale. Use a one-inch-to-one-foot ratio.

If sketching, use a pencil, eraser, and plain paper. Keep all your preliminary sketches, compare and evaluate them, and choose the best—all before you begin to think about color.

If a design is good, color may improve it. But color will never improve a poor design.

Work on an idea and then put it away for a while. The delay enables you to view the whole idea from a distance and share it with others who can critique it.

Ideas for designs do not all come at once. They may come from bits and pieces of experience. Allow enough time for your design to develop.

Where do ideas come from?

Clippings from magazines, catalogs, junk mail
Photographs
Illustrations from children's books
Greeting cards, postcards
A character or event in a book you are reading
Found objects
Commemoration of a person, relationship
Designs in commercial fabric
Observing people, animals
Writings from your journal
Listening to music
An event you've observed or participated in

A resource file of subjects for design can be very helpful. I keep mine in a large three-ring binder, with the clippings in page protectors sorted by subjects. Some libraries also keep files of clippings you can check out.

Think about what draws you to certain images. Is it the color, interesting details, strong composition? This analysis will give you some clues as to what direction your designs should take.

Here are some design exercises to get you started.

Exercise One: Doodle in the Box

What you will need:

Copies of the small boxes page *(see p. 24)*
Pencil
Eraser

Many times our hands and mind are most free when we are doodling during a phone conversation, during a meeting, while waiting. These doodles are a good place to start designing. The small boxes break up the intimidating blank page. Start with one of your initials. Without stopping and analyzing, fill up as many boxes as you can design with different renditions of your initial. When you come to a stop, put the

For pictorial or home furnishings designs, start by doodling in small boxes. The theme of the doodle sheet above were the letters N, C, S. When you are designing clothing, draw the shape of the garment and doodle within the garment shape. Printable copies of these and additional design templates can be downloaded from the CD-ROM.

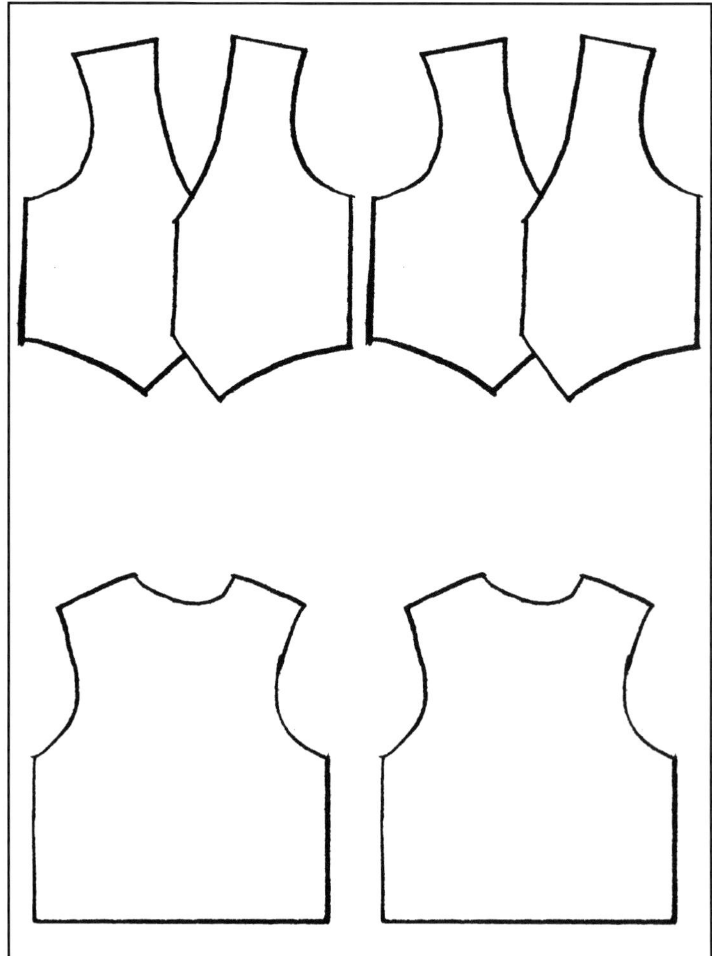

doodle page away for a day or more. When you come back to it, choose the most interesting doodle box and draw more variations of it to fill the remaining boxes on the page or start an entire new page.

Think about: orientation of the initial in the box; repetition; rotating and flipping the initial; positive and negative space.

Some weavers have created their business card or a moniker to sign their work while doing this exercise. You may want to use all of your initials together and repeat this exercise.

I often start the design process this way, doing dozens of doodles. If I'm designing a wall hanging, the boxes are proportionate to the size of the finished piece.

Exercise Two: Torn paper collage

What you will need:

- A variety of papers: newsprint, magazine ads, construction paper, art papers, gift wrap
- Glue stick
- A heavy blank sheet of paper, white or black at least 8½″ x 11″
- Tracing paper
- Fine point black marker
- Copy machine
- Color medium

Tear images from paper and work within the framework of a square or rectangle background sheet. Arrange the shapes to make a pleasing composition. When you have achieved a good composition, lay a piece of tracing paper over it and trace the edges of the design elements using a fine point black marker. Leave out fussy details. Make several copies of this design to experiment with color.

The example here is a composition emphasizing the idea of growth. The lines in this composition seem to move from the bottom of the square to the top. Note the repetition of leaf forms and the organic lines of the torn paper edges. This design could be woven crossways; the pattern weft picks would then run up and down when the piece is turned to hang vertically.

A torn paper collage is another way to evolve a design using forms and color.

Exercise Three: Found object collage

What you need:

- Copy machine or computer scanner
- Plain paper
- Found objects
- Color medium

Another way to create a design is to start with an idea or theme. Walk around your living/working space and pick up objects that will fit on your copier or scanner. Use the copier to record different combinations until you have one that you like.

Composition is important. Fill the space, but avoid the temptation to include too much. If you become frustrated, try removing some pieces. You might want to include a focal point to draw the eye to a specific place in your composition. I like to work in black and white mode on the copier or computer printer. When you have achieved a pleasing composition, lay a piece of tracing paper over it and trace the edges of the design elements using a fine point black marker. Leave out fussy details. Make several copies of this design to experiment with color.

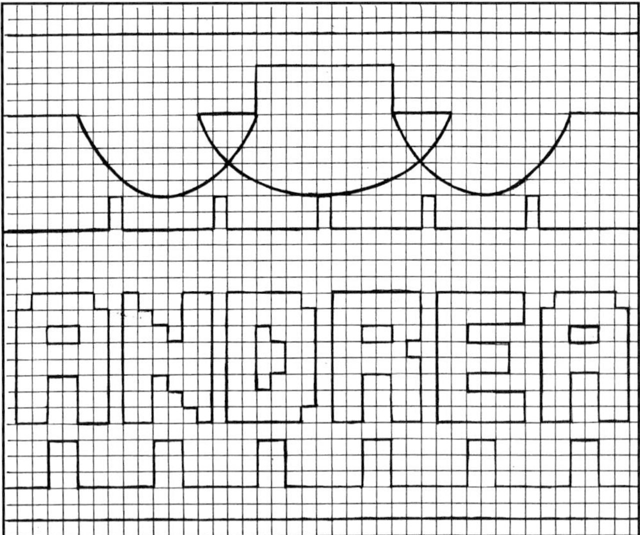

A grid is another way to develop a design. In this example, the grid is a map for a design based on a name.

Exercise Four: Starting with a grid

What you will need:

Graph paper
No. 2B pencil
Eraser
Colored pencils or markers

In this design, graph paper is used to map out letters of a name. Line is one of the most important elements of design. Here, other lines—diagonal and curved—have been added to create an interesting composition. These curved lines begin to exploit the potential of this design-weave structure.

Another aspect of design is positive and negative space. In this name design, the positive spaces show as the darkest and lightest areas; they could be woven using contrasting pattern wefts. The negative space is the area of the ground fabric that is not covered by either pattern weft. This negative space will be outlined by the turnarounds of pattern weft, taking advantage of another aspect of the weave structure.

Contrasting color is also an important design element. The choice for the letters should be a color that provides a contrast to the color of the ground fabric. Color choices for other areas defined by the lines in this design should be harmonious with this main color. Fill in these different areas with color to see how the finished piece will look. You may want to make copies and try several different color schemes.

You have now used straight and curved lines, positive and negative space, and color, in our experiments with designing for this weave structure.

Exercise Five: Reproducing realistic imagery

What you need:

Copier or scanner
Photo of landscape
Fine point black marker

Another approach to design involves reproducing realistic imagery, such as a photo or drawing. The example is a postcard photograph of a landscape. Find a landscape that interests you. Reduce or enlarge the image to 8½x 11 inches on a copier or scanner. Copy or convert the image to black and white. Emphasize the lines of mountains, hills, water, clouds, animals, trees using a fine point black marker. You can ignore elements you don't want to include. The landscape has predominately horizontal lines, and the direction of the weaving will reinforce these lines. If the landscape were composed primarily of vertical lines, such as tree trunks, then it would be better to exploit the weave structure by weaving it sideways.

The Moorman technique lends itself best to designs with flat areas of color. The illusion of a third dimension is difficult to achieve. Nonetheless, there are some ways to suggest perspective. Lines that converge into the distance draw the viewer's eye into the composi-

This picture postcard became the basis for a realistic design.

tion. Larger objects appear to be close, and diminishing sizes suggest that objects are farther away. Shapes that overlap also suggest depth. Another way to fool the eye into seeing depth is to use color gradation. Stronger colors appear closer; fading color and less distinct lines indicate distance.

Exercise Six: Creating abstract compositions

What you need:

- Watercolor paper
- Watercolor paints or bottles of colored ink
- Several paint brushes
- Water
- Fine point black marker
- Two pieces of **L**-shaped cardboard

You may wish to create a completely non-objective composition. Perhaps you want to include color relationships in the design process from the outset, or you wish to design a piece with simple, flowing lines. Try making a loose watercolor or ink wash to express your feelings while listening to music. As the colors flow together and blend, you will find that certain areas of your painting are more interesting.

To make a watercolor wash, you will need a cup of water and a large paint brush. Apply a generous amount of water to the paper. Using other brushes, dip and float colors into the water wash. Tip and let run. Let the wash dry and see what part of it you like.

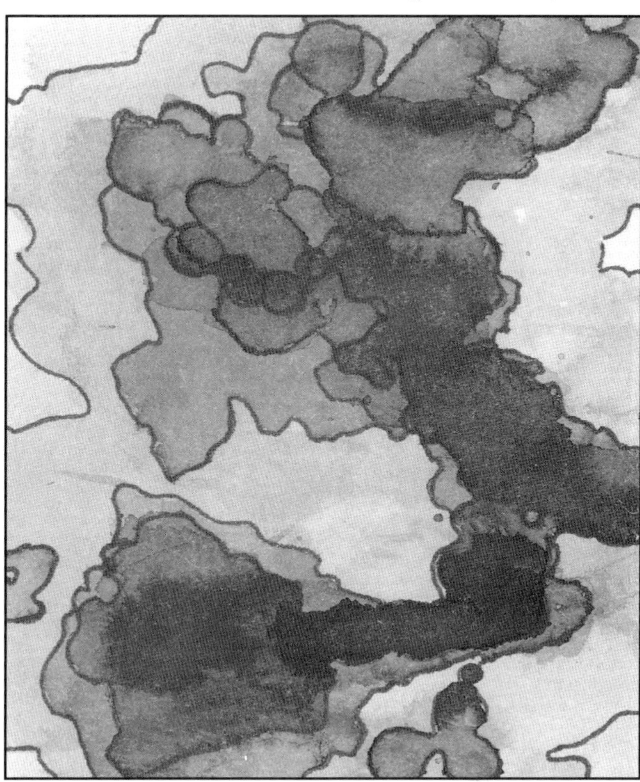

Abstract compositions can be created by making a watercolor wash.

Look for movement and direction. Try to include a focal point, perhaps an area of special interest or strong, contrasting color. When the painting is dry, use a black marker to emphasize the main shapes. Take two **L**-shaped cardboard strips and frame areas of your work until you find a strong composition. Look for balance as well, with areas to be woven all across the piece. This consideration is both technical and artistic. If the tie-down yarns are not used over large areas, these areas will develop looser tension as the weaving progresses. Curved, flowing lines can be woven, but curves must be long enough to progress evenly under the spaced tie-down threads.

Exercise Seven: Starting from fabric designs

What you need:

- One-eighth yard quilt or clothing fabric
- Copy machine or scanner
- Tracing or graph paper, or sketch pad

Take a trip to your local fabric shop or quilt store, or maybe you already have a stash of fabric on hand. Look for fabric that has appealing designs that lend themselves to weaving.

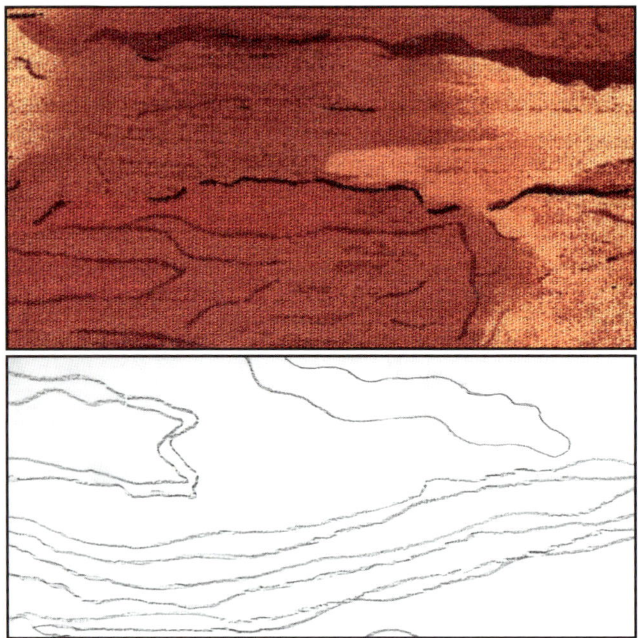

This design was taken from commercial quilt fabric and translated to a cartoon.

Examine the motifs and design elements of the pattern printed on the fabric. Rhythm and repetition are the building blocks of most fabric design. Isolate one shape or motif and play around with it. You might start by sketching in the doodle boxes or on graph paper as you manipulate and change the motif. Or you might trace the motif directly with tracing paper or use a copy machine or scanner to capture the motif.

When weaving pillows or clothing, Joyce often uses the fabric that inspired the design to line clothing or back the pillow.

Ethnic designs

Often a good place to start the search for symbols and designs that have personal meaning is in your ethnic heritage. Today, unfortunately, ethnic is "in," so many designs have been stolen by trendy culture. The meaning of the symbolism and colors have sometimes been lost in the quest for "style." When examining your own culture or one you have adopted, discover what is meaningful for you in the symbol. Look at the historical and cultural background. Then find a way to make your own statement, not copying the symbol directly, but interpreting the symbol for yourself.

Replica of a Zuni pot from Joyce Harter collection

Traditional ethnic textiles and pottery are a source of ideas. They often use repeated patterns. Native American pottery designs are particularly rich in motifs that combine lines and circular shapes such as the Theo Moorman technique can produce. This replica of a Zuni pot shows a combination of circular and linear shapes that often characterizes ethnic design.

Using color

Color is important in the design process. Developing your own sense of color is important for weaving any structure. Learning the formal language of color is a good place to start. Several resources for color theory are the numerous books by Wucius Wong, including *Principles of Color Design.* Or you might look at *Designing for Weaving: A Study Guide for Drafting, Design and Color* by Carol Kurtz. Some weavers get stuck using the same colors over and over. Think about your relationship to colors. Why do you like certain colors and hate others? What could you learn if you picked two colors you dislike and used them in your next design? The following books will help you visualize your favorite colors in new combinations.

Color Harmony: A Guide to Creative Color Combinations by Hideaki Chijiiwa

Understanding Color An Introduction for Designers by Linda Holtzschue

A postcard of The Flower Window by Carl Larsson is the basis for this color wrapping.

Pantone Guide to Communicating with Color by Leatrice Eiseman.

Exercise Eight: Color wrapping

What you need:

Object from nature
Matte board
Assortment of yarns
Double-sided tape

Find an object from nature—a shell, stone, fruit, or a vegetable. Look at the object from all angles in bright daylight or with full spectrum light. Analyze and dissect all the colors your eye can see in that object. Use yarns from your stash at home or take a trip to the yarn store. Cut a strip of matte board one inch wide and eight inches long. Cut lengths of yarn that represent the colors in the object. Wrap the yarn around the matte board securing it on the back side with double-stick tape. As your eye gets more attuned to seeing all the colors in natural objects, you can use a variety of yarn textures to help represent the feeling of the object. You can also wrap yarns in widths proportionate to the amount of individual colors in the object.

Here the colors in a seashell form the basis for the wrapping.

Colors never stand alone; they are always surrounded by other colors. Since the tie-down warp is a very fine thread and the pattern inlay weft sits on the surface of the ground, showing through in its full intensity, the color and texture of the yarns used in the Theo Moorman technique take on a special importance. Using a simple group of three or four colors that are next to each other on the color wheel gives a work unity. A small shape of an unusual color can provide a focal point. Even white and black must be taken into consideration here. A white warp, often thought of as neutral, will turn bright pattern inlay weft colors into washed-out tints, while a black warp will bring out the sparkle of strong hues.

Coloring a scale drawing with colored pencils, design markers, watercolors, pastels or a computer design program, will help you decide what colors to use in executing a design. As you try colors you may want to refer to the yarns in your studio. Of course, several yarns can be used together. A vibrant effect can be achieved by winding several yarns of different tone and texture on one shuttle for the pattern weft. Blending and gradating yarns in this way adds richness to the weaving.

The next step is to visualize your design as woven cloth.

Chapter 5

Visualizing Your Design in Theo Moorman

Weaving that sings combines good design and successful weaving. Good design employs the elements of line, space, contrast, composition, pattern, and color. This chapter discusses these aspects of design, applying them specifically to pieces woven in the Theo Moorman technique. Successful weaving means that the design takes advantage of the structure, and the structure enhances the design.

Evaluating a design

The first step is to ask if a design is suitable for weaving or whether it would be better rendered in some other art form?

As you grow in your design capabilities, you will find some great ideas that won't work in weaving as well as they might in a quilt, a painting, a sculpture, or a collage of mixed media. If you have a great design that needs to come to life, but weaving isn't the right medium, consider collaborating with another artist who can render your design in another medium. (In return you can weave a piece for them.) You can learn much from explaining and clarifying your vision with another artist.

Another possibility is that your design is suited for weaving, but will need a non-woven element to complete it, such as a carved wooden hanging device or a welded form on which to drape the weaving, or electronic wizardry to make pieces move in an installation. Here collaboration with other creative people is a must. In addition, figuring out how the piece will need to be finished, while you are still in the design phase, can save you many headaches later on.

Theo Moorman or not?

The next step is to decide if the design will work in the Theo Moorman technique.

Special considerations apply when you are creating pictorial weaving in this technique. For example, the intricate connections that characterize traditional tapestry weaving are not present in the Moorman technique, so a design with small figures may be better realized in traditional tapestry. All-over designs may be better realized in a loom-controlled fabric. The turnaround of the pattern inlay yarns at the edges of the design elements must be considered as part of the design. The ground fabric is an element in the structure of the piece and in the evolution of the design.

Following are some questions to ask when you are deciding whether or not your design will work in Moorman. For a complete list of designing questions, download Designing Worksheet from the CD-ROM.

For a wall hanging you might ask: Will the piece hang vertically or horizontally?

Are the design elements large enough to be held in place by the tie-downs? How will the design look from a distance? Close up? What kind of device will support the wall hanging? Will this device show, and thus influence the design, or be invisible?

For clothing in the Moorman technique you might ask: Where will the design elements be placed on the garment? What kinds of yarns will give the drape and weight of fabric desired? Will the garment be lined or unlined? Will it be reversible? Will the entire garment be handwoven or should some woven panels be combined with commercial fabric? What adornment—buttons, trim, beads—does the garment need to make it sing?

For a Moorman one-sided rug you might ask: How will the design transfer to the rug? Will the rug be used on the floor or hang on a wall? If the rug is going to be used on the floor, does the design invite stepping on or stepping around? How will the ends of the rug be finished?

For double warp overlay rugs or runners you might ask: Do I want to use both sides? How are the two sides of the weaving related to each other? Do they complement or contrast?

Adapting your design to cloth

As you evaluate your design, it will help to think about some of the design options that this weave offers. Some examples of these options are shown in the gallery on the next two pages.

As you work with the Moorman technique, its structure will influence your designs, and your designs will influence your use of the weave. The more familiar you are with the way this weave works, the more possibilities you will see in it.

text continues on page 34

DETAIL, ALTAR HANGING GRACE LUTHERAN CHURCH SCHENECTADY, NEW YORK

It is possible to make a striking design by letting the background fabric be the design area. Inlay pattern weft over the entire weaving except in the design areas. You may need to modify your design to keep the positive and negative areas balanced. JH

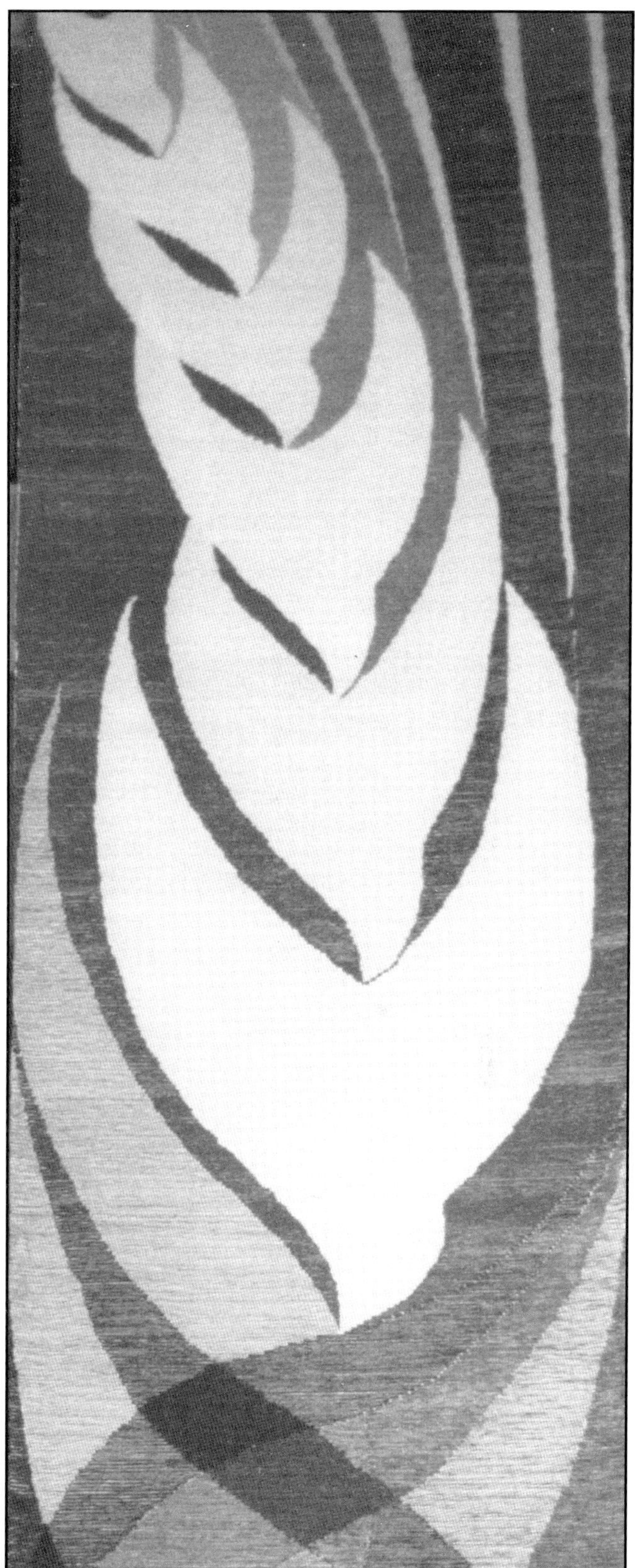

DESCENDING DOVE, WALL HANGING UNITED LUTHERAN CHURCH, RED WING, MN **4′ x 14′**

Repetition of a shape in many subtle color changes makes a dramatic design element and is another way to add an appearance of depth to a composition. JH

A Gallery of Moorman Design Possibilities

23RD PSALM 6′ x 3′
You do not need to be limited by the width of the loom. Wall hangings can be woven lengthwise to hang crosswise. The weft, which is dominant on the loom because it is covered only by the lightweight tie-down warp, will become a dominant vertical if the piece is hung sideways. JH

EARTH CLAY 32″ x 36″
The Moorman weave adapts easily to lettering. Letters can be rendered either positively or negatively. That is, they can be woven with the pattern weft or everything but the letters can be woven so that the ground fabric forms the writing. Here, letters have been woven with the pattern weft. JH

PURPLE SWAN VEST, **detail** *(see p. 70)*
One of the joys of Moorman is that subtle curves are possible. By using a cartoon on the surface and following it carefully, you can create gently curved shapes. The line may appear slightly jagged when viewed on the loom, but from a distance it will be seen as a curve. A sense of movement can be enhanced by bleeding the colors of one curve into the next. JH

Fall Equinox Vest, **detail** *(see p. 66)*

Isolated fine points and narrow lines can be prominent design elements. To create a narrow line on the surface of the fabric, carry a pattern weft from one tie-down to another, as in the web connecting these leaves. A pattern weft travels from one tie-down to another. In some rows, the same tie-down warp is picked up and encircled by the pattern weft, even if it isn't supposed to be raised for that row. The jagged line appears much smoother when the vest is viewed from a distance. NS

The Earth, The Air, The Fire, The Water Return **29″ x 25″**

In this example, the ground warps and tie-down warps were painted with the same dyes in order to make the tie-downs seem to disappear. NS

Detail, wall hanging, First English Lutheran Church, Cannon Falls, MN

A shadow can be used to emphasize an area of the design or to add depth. Shadow effects can be woven with a different shade of pattern weft. JH

Choice of color in warp

As you design a piece of cloth in the Moorman weave, you must make many choices about color. The color of the ground warp will affect your composition. If you warp with two cones, you can increase the intensity of color in the ground warp by blending two closely related colors. Winding a warp by twos makes no difference in the way the yarns lie in the warp after they are threaded through the heddles.

Here are some other ways to vary the warp. Choose one color and gradate the value of the warp from light to dark from one edge to the other as you wind. Or choose two or three hues that sit next to each other on the color wheel and progress through them from one edge of the warp to the other. Using these color schemes, you could create subtle or blatant warp stripes as you wind the warp.

Make a mixed warp using a warping paddle. For further information see *Winding Multi-Colored Warps with a Warping Paddle* by Leslie Voiers. One of my favorite student warps is a mixture of six different yellow cottons. For weft, choose a yarn that is the most neutral (neither the most saturated nor the lightest nor the darkest value) of the bunch of warp yarns.

Tie-down warp

Even more choices present themselves when it comes to choosing the tie-down warp.

The tie-down warp does not have to be wound with just one color. I often use two or more colors of tie-down warp in my weavings. One color can be the same as the ground warp, while the second color is several shades lighter or darker.

You can also use contrasting colors in the tie-down warp. This trick is especially useful if you are working with a black or white ground warp. It makes the tie-down warp much easier to see against the ground when you are weaving. Contrasting colored tie-downs also add a design element to the ground fabric in areas where there is no pattern inlay.

If your ground warp color is dark but many of

A contrasting tie-down warp is easier to see when adding pattern inlay. It also adds interest to the fabric where there is inlaid design.

your pattern inlay yarns are light, another option is to wind the tie-down warp with areas of light color where most of the design elements fall. This choice can enhance the brightness of your design.

Mercerized 20/2 cotton has a sheen and will add some vibrancy to the fabric. Unmercerized 20/2 cotton will almost disappear when used with unmercerized cotton or wool ground warp yarn. New World Textiles is an excellent source of unmercerized 20/2 cotton.

If you want the tie-down yarns to be a strong design element in the piece, there are several options. You can use variegated tie-down yarns in bold colors in contrast to the ground and pattern inlay. A black warp with a variegated tie-down could be striking. However, the availability of commercial space-dyed yarns in the 20/2 size is limited. There are some variegated threads used for sewing machine embroidery and embellishment that may be strong enough for tie-down warp. See Resources for embroidery thread information. To create your own variegated tie-down, you can dye paint a neutral-colored warp. An excellent reference, although written for the quilting world, is *Color by Design: Paint and Print with Dye* by Ann Johnston. Or with a warping paddle, wind four to eight different colored cones of yarn together. I prefer making multi-colored warps for much of my weaving and find a warping paddle invaluable.

Another way to emphasize the tie-down warps is to increase the size of yarn used. The most commonly used size is 20/2. However, going to 8/2, 10/2, or even 5/2 will bring the tie-down warp to the forefront and create strong vertical lines in the design.

Woven wire might also be used for a tie-down. On a small scale, certain copper, brass, or other jewelry wires could work.

On the other hand, here are at least four ways to make the tie-down warp blend in or disappear.

Use a neutral gray tie-down warp.

Use an even narrower diameter tie-down yarn, 30/3 silk for example. Make sure your silk or rayon is resilient enough at these fine sizes.

Dye-paint a neutral colored warp in the same colors as the ground warp.

Experiment with monofilament for the tie-down. Monofilament is difficult to work with, but it is "invisible" and strong enough for tie-down warp. Your local fishing store may have other materials as well. Certain types of clear machine quilting threads will also work.

A chart of suggested warp materials and yarn characteristics can be found on page 107.

Weft yarn variations

Experimentation is the key. For a very firm fabric your weft would be the same as the warp. But if you want an opaque fabric that has some drape, you can play with ground weft.

For example, you can create a secondary background pattern in your design by adding interest to the ground. Weft that is space-dyed and variegated—cotton, silk, wool yarns, and chenilles (both cotton and rayon)—brings a lot of spice to the ground fabric. Such wefts also can mask the color of the warp, so you can make one warp and, by changing weft yarns, weave two pieces that appear totally different from the same warp.

Use two or three strands of weft yarns wound together on one shuttle so the weft is larger in diameter than the warp. This will cause the weaving to become more weft-faced. This is another way to mask a warp.

If you want more texture in the ground, try a slubby yarn or a tweedy yarn. Try a weft material unrelated to the warp (wool warp with rayon weft; cotton warp with silk noil weft; linen warp with Tencel weft). Use fabric strips cut to ¼-inch as ground weft. Blend two or more yarns of different textures together for the ground weft (a flake cotton with a mercerized cotton).

To play with color, try a weft yarn of the same intensity as the warp but a different hue (a black warp with a deep purple weft). Or try a weft yarn of the same hue as the warp, but a lighter or darker value. Try a weft yarn in a complementary color to the warp. Create contrast by winding a warm and cool color together on the same shuttle.

If you are comfortable with dyeing, dye-paint the warp and use a solid color weft or vice versa. Or dye-paint both the warp and the weft yarns. Ikat dye the weft and use a solid color in the warp or vice versa. Ikat dye both the warp and weft.

When you have let your imagination play with your design to visualize ways in which it might be woven, then you are ready to begin the process of finalizing it in a cartoon to be used as a road map for your weaving.

Chapter 6

Technical Tips

While many weavers need to create a full-scale design on paper and translate it directly to the loom, some weavers prefer to work much more loosely. If you are comfortable with making design choices while you weave, your process of adapting your design to the cloth will be very different from the process described in this chapter. Both processes are valid ways of working in the Moorman technique. The intuition and experience required for working organically can not be written about easily. Those of you who have the capability to design and translate at the loom have a gift! Weavers who are more comfortable making all the decisions before starting to weave can experience this looser way of working by trying the Weave Play exercise at the end of this chapter.

Enlarging your design

The first step in translating your thumbnail sketch or scale drawing is enlarging the design.

To translate a small design to a large design you must decide what scale you are using. It is necessary to allow for take-up in weaving and shrinkage. If you need a five-foot finished rug, you must weave it longer on the loom. The place to allow for this take-up is on the full-scale enlargement. Not only will the piece be woven longer, but also the design will be elongated. Once woven, the design will appear normal because of loom take-up. For rugs, wall hangings, pillows, and table runners I usually add one inch per foot in the length. Thus my scale is one inch equals a thirteen-inch foot.

Giving exact ratios is difficult, because shrinkage will vary from project to project depending on the yarns used, the sett, the weaver's beat and the length of the design. Usually one inch per lengthwise foot is sufficient. On a grid, each one-inch square of the design will become thirteen inches (warp-direction) when enlarged. It benefits the weaver to keep track of how much shrinkage occurs on each project. Compare the completed weaving to the full-scale design. These records will give you a "yardstick" for future projects.

For clothing, add the length to the pattern pieces at the alteration lines marked on the pattern. For clothing I usually add one and one-half inch per foot to accommodate not only loom take-up, but also additional shrinkage when the fabric is washed and steam pressed before sewing.

There is not so much take-up in width, so the design can be drawn the same width as the finished design for weavings less than three feet wide. The width of a warp in a piece wider than thirty-six inches should be about two inches wider than the design to allow for draw-in in the weaving. Using a temple when you are weaving will help maintain the desired width of the fabric.

Here are ways to enlarge a drawing.

1. Use an opaque projector or presentation software on a computer to throw the design on a wall and trace around it. Kopykake makes a number of excellent copy projectors for crafters. See Resources.

2. Take the design to a copy service center. If you bring the design in on paper, they can scan and digitize it for you. Most full service centers can copy up to thirty-six inches wide and as long as you need. (Length is limited only by the length of the copy paper roll.) A black and white copy is sufficient since the weaver adds the color later.

3. Scan the design into a computer graphics or photo editing program and enlarge it to the correct size. Print the design in segments on

8½″ x 11″ paper and tape the pages together to form the full-scale design.

4. Grid the design with pencil, ruler, and paper. I prefer this low-tech version of enlarging because you don't need any special equipment.

Gridding a design

Draw grid marks on the small-scale design. If your small-scale design is drawn on graph paper, use the special knitters' graph paper that has the elongated boxes. *Graph It* by Gail Selfridge is one resource for reproducible graph paper. The next step is to grid full-sized drawing paper with light pencil marks to show the squares that match the ones on the small design. If the suggestion on the preceding page is followed, each square on the drawing paper will be twelve inches wide and thirteen inches tall. Next translate the designs in the small squares to the scale of the large squares; look closely at each small square and copy all the lines in it to the corresponding large square. This enlarged design shows the outlines of the shapes you will be weaving. Darken the design lines with a black permanent marker, (I use the Sharpie brand) so they can be seen easily. If yarn choices are complete, then the colors for each design segment can be indicated by coloring with corresponding colored markers, or written in, or a sample of yarns to be used in each design area can be taped to the paper.

Joyce transfers the design from the original to the cartoon.

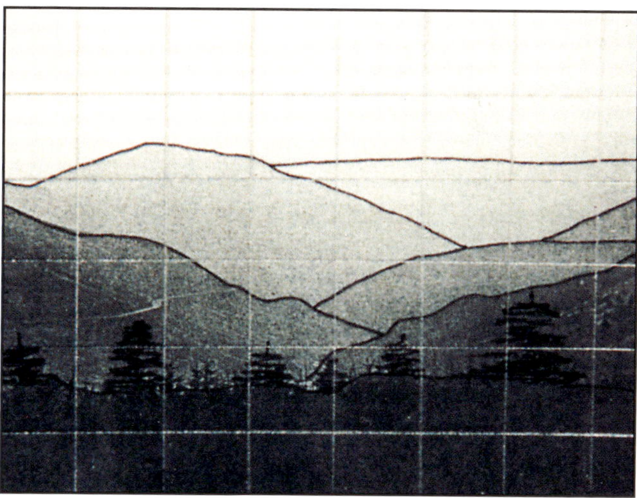

The design is gridded for transfer to the cartoon.

Trace the design from the paper enlargement onto the featherweight cartoon using color markers. The drawing on the featherweight fabric will be the same size as the large paper drawing of the design.

Cartoon on the top

In her liturgical weaving business, Joyce needed to have her designs produced at the loom exactly as she had drawn them. Making a cartoon was a logical step in producing work for churches. Early in her career, Joyce had used a cartoon to place embroidery upon handwoven cloth. Familiarity with the hand-embroidery method of following a design from a cartoon on the surface led her to make a cartoon to attach to the top of the fabric when she began to weave in the Theo Moorman technique.

This practical way to have a cartoon constantly visible delights all weavers who learn it, far outweighing the traditional use of a paper cartoon underneath, or drawing on the warp. The cartoon is sewn to the surface of the weaving and flipped back. The weaver inlays between the lines of the design following the backside of the cartoon. Some weavers may not like having their work covered as they weave, but the accuracy gained from following the design far outweighs not being able to see the work. Using a cartoon this way requires that all decisions about designs and yarn colors be made before the weaving begins.

Making the cartoon

Use non-fusible, non-woven, featherweight interfacing fabric. It is a pliable, non-raveling material normally used to stiffen garments for sewing. It is transparent so that you can see the lines you have drawn through it. It will stay rolled on the fell of your fabric where shuttles can lie on it. Heavier interfacing will not work as well because it is not transparent and is too stiff. Most brands of featherweight interfacing stretch in one direction. Check the direction of stretch. Place the stretch warpwise (lengthwise). Interfacing purchased from a fabric store will normally be 22 inches wide. For large designs, it can be pieced with a glue stick. For 48-inch wide fabric, see Resources.

1. Cut a piece of featherweight interfacing the same width and slightly longer than the full-size drawing.
2. Place it over the paper drawing with the sides of the drawing even with the edges of the interfacing cartoon with the extra length extending at the bottom. Use pattern weights or silverware to hold the interfacing in place on top of the paper design.
3. Using a quilting ruler, draw a straight black line across the interfacing one inch from the bottom. (Quilting rulers are made of clear, heavy plastic, ruled in quarter-inch sections and come in a variety of widths. The six-inch -wide ruler is my favorite.) Place the bottom of the paper cartoon on this line.
4. Trace the designs from the paper onto the transparent interfacing. Use the same black permanent marker used for the paper design.
5. Areas of color are filled in or outlined with colored permanent markers that correspond to the colors of the yarns you will be using. I like the Berol Permacolor art markers that have a fine point on one end and a broad point on the other end. Do not use a washable children's marker or a kind you are unsure of. The cartoon rolls onto the cloth beam along with the woven fabric. You do not want the cartoon to bleed onto the woven fabric or have the color rub off onto your fingers as you weave.

For cartoons wider than twenty-four inches, draw a dashed black line vertically down the center of the cartoon. This line will help keep the cartoon aligned to the center of the warp. I mark the center of my reed with a brightly colored yarn.

Basting the cartoon to the fabric

Begin by weaving two to five inches of plain weave, depending on the depth of your hem. With the right side of the cartoon up, line up the solid black line at the bottom of the cartoon with the fell line of the fabric. The fell line is where the unwoven warp meets the woven fabric; it advances with each pick. Using quilting thread and a large needle (some weavers use a curved upholstery needle—see Resources), baste the cartoon to the weaving two or three rows back from the fell line using long running stitches.

Baste the cartoon, to the fabric, right side up, below the black fell line you have drawn on the cartoon.

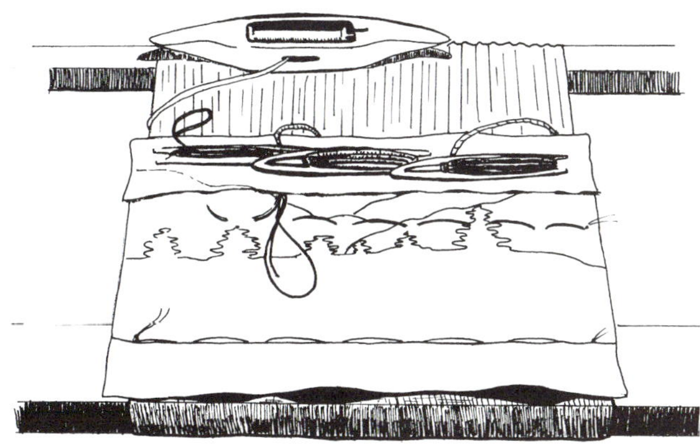

Featherweight interfacing usually stretches lengthwise. Re-baste the cartoon every six to eight inches to insure accurate placement of the design.

The cartoon is now stitched down and covering up your warp. Flip the cartoon back towards you. Roll up the excess cartoon and use a straight pin on each edge to hold the rolled up cartoon together. As you weave, you are following the back side of the cartoon. Inlay between the design lines. The fact that the cartoon is transparent allows you to see both the design and the colors. Each row, advance the cartoon so it stays at the fell line. It may be helpful to place a lease stick, yardstick, or stick shuttle at the fell line on top of the cartoon and underneath the flipped back portion to keep the cartoon exactly at the fell line. If you are using a temple to keep your warp stretched, it can be placed on top of the sewed down portion of the cartoon and underneath the flipped back portion of the cartoon to help keep the cartoon in place. Re-baste the cartoon to the completed design every six to eight inches to keep it securely in place. Stretch the cartoon as you stitch it down. This interval stitching is extremely important, especially for an intricate design. The cartoon continues to roll onto the cloth beam with the fabric and is not removed until the fabric has been cut from the loom.

Working with two warp beams

Both authors weave on Macomber looms equipped with a second warp beam and back beam. Most commercial floor looms will accommodate a second warp beam. Your loom manufacturer can tell you if it is possible to add one to your loom. For the Moorman technique, it is best if the second beam is a plain beam.

While it is possible to weave the Moorman technique on only one beam, there are definite advantages to working on a loom with two warp

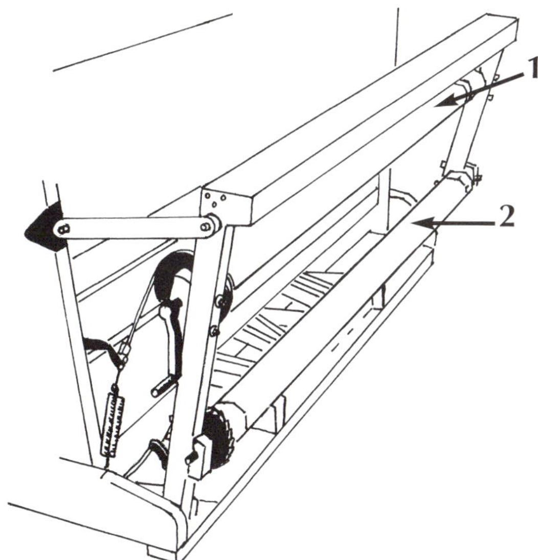

A loom with two warp beams is an advantage in the Theo Moorman technique.

beams. A warp over three yards long often develops unequal tension between the tie-down and ground warps. The advantage of two warp beams for a long warp is that the tie-down yarns can be beamed separately and the tension adjusted on each set of warp yarns while you are weaving. Even if the design areas on the weaving are not proportionately spaced, the two sets of warp yarns will help keep an even tension.

What to do if you have only one back beam

If you only have one beam available, then keep the following in mind:

Plan projects less than three yards long; warp for one project at a time.

Avoid creating a design where the design areas are disproportionately spaced (for example, all the inlay in the center of the cloth).

Always wind the tie-down and the ground warps separately.

Warp from back to front, using a pair of lease sticks for each warp.

Lift shafts 3 and 4 to raise the tie-down warps to the surface before tying on and tensioning.

Warping the loom

The authors recommend warping from back to front for this technique. If you warp from front to back, follow your normal warping procedures.

Warping on two beams is somewhat different from warping with a single beam. The ground warp and the tie-down warp are wound separately; the heavier ground warp is wound first and set aside. Then the tie-down warp is wound.

For wall hangings, Joyce omits the last tie-down yarn on the right hand side; for tie-downs, measure one less than half the number of yarns in the ground warp.

For clothing tie-downs, measure half the number of yarns in the ground warp.

For double warp overlay tie-downs, (rugs, table runners) measure a number equal to the ground warp.

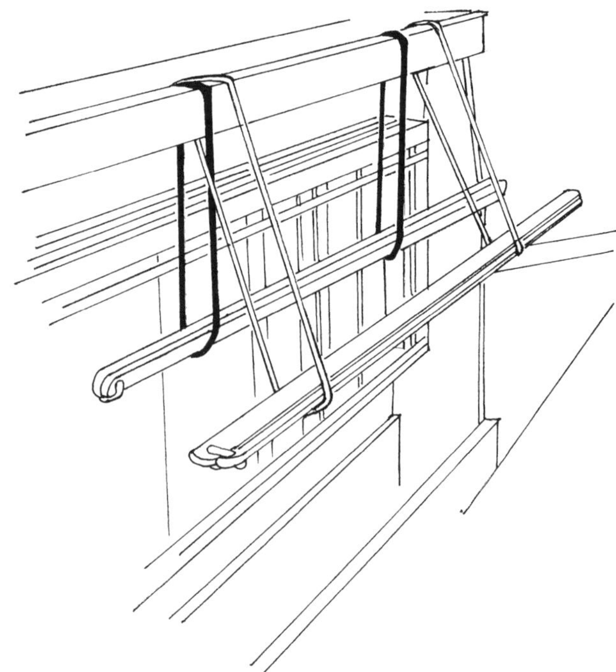

Two sets of lease sticks can be suspended from the castle of the loom.

Add the second back beam before winding the second warp onto the lower warp beam. The two sets of lease sticks allow the tie-down warp to ride on top of the ground warp.
The second set of lease sticks goes through the cross in the tie-down warp and rides in a pair of string cradles hanging from the castle of the loom. Spread this warp in the raddle. Roll the tie-down warp onto the lower, or second, warp beam adding a separating material. Both sets of lease sticks will remain in place until the loom is threaded.

Warping back to front with two warp beams

You need two sets of lease sticks. The first set goes through the cross of the ground warp and rides in a pair of string cradles hanging from the castle of the loom. Spread this warp in a raddle and roll it onto the top warp beam of your loom adding separating material (paper or sticks). Most looms with a second warp beam also have a second back beam. Put the second back beam on the loom after you have rolled on the ground warp.

Warping back to front with one warp beam

Put one pair of lease sticks through the ground warp cross. Put the second pair of lease sticks through the tie-down warp cross. Hang the warps from the two sets of string cradles. Spread the warps in the raddle. Then bind supplementary rods that have been slipped through the uncut ends of both warps separately to the back beam rod with shoestrings. Each warp has its own rod. Roll both warps together onto the warp beam.

Threading the loom

Threading the heddles of a floor loom will be easier if you can lower the breast beam and beater or get inside that space. Sit on a small stool or chair inside the loom so that your eye level is near the level of the heddle eyes. With two sets of lease sticks on the back of your loom, one above the other, you will be able to see to thread the heavier yarns in the shafts 1 and 2 and the finer yarns in shafts 3 and 4. Once they are threaded, lift shafts 3 and 4 to raise the tie-down warps to the surface before tying on and tensioning.

For more warping tips, and directions for warping two beams, see *Warping On a Shoestring* in Resources.

Troubleshooting

Things can go wrong no matter how carefully you are weaving. Below are a few remedies Joyce developed to correct problems.

Avoiding unwanted stripes

When weaving with two or more shuttles carrying different colored yarns in the same tie-down shed, it is very important to keep the shuttles in sequence. If the color order does not stay the same, stripes will occur where blending was

Stripes rather than blending will occur when a consistent shuttle sequence is not maintained. The error is apparent in the central flame of this weaving where both stripes and a vague fuzzy area are visible.

desired. Maintaining a consistent shuttle sequence all the way through the crossover design areas will prevent you from making an error that cannot be repaired.

Straight selvage

To keep a straight selvage, pinch the edge warp yarn with your thumb and forefinger while tugging on the shuttle carrying the ground weft. Use either a bubble or an angle in the weft to prevent draw-in. A temple can be used to maintain width.

Missing a row

An error that can occur, especially on a wide piece, is that you may not see that you have missed an area of inlay. It is possible to lift the tie-down yarns in the previous row to lay in a pattern weft, even though you have placed the ground weft and beaten it into place. However, this correction cannot be made more than one

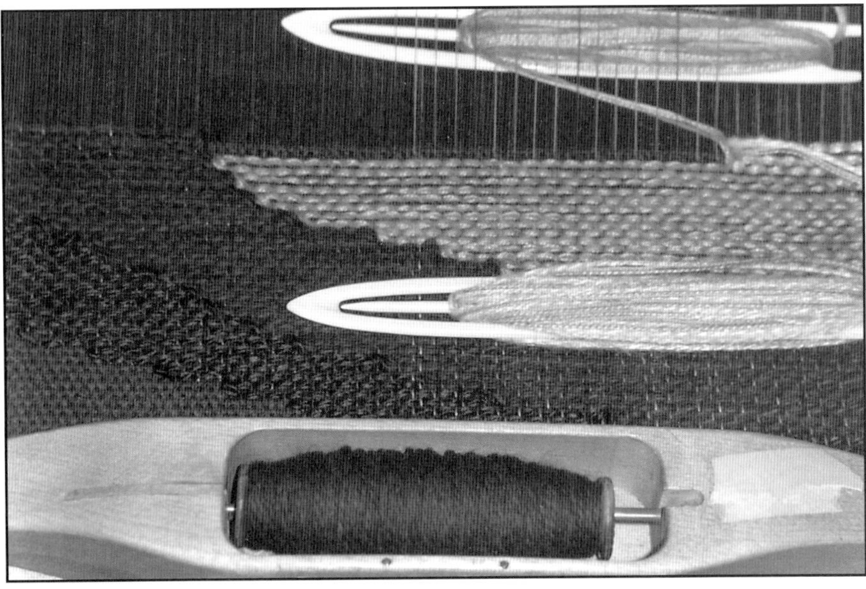

You can lift tie-down threads to insert a row of pattern weft that you have missed, but only one row back.

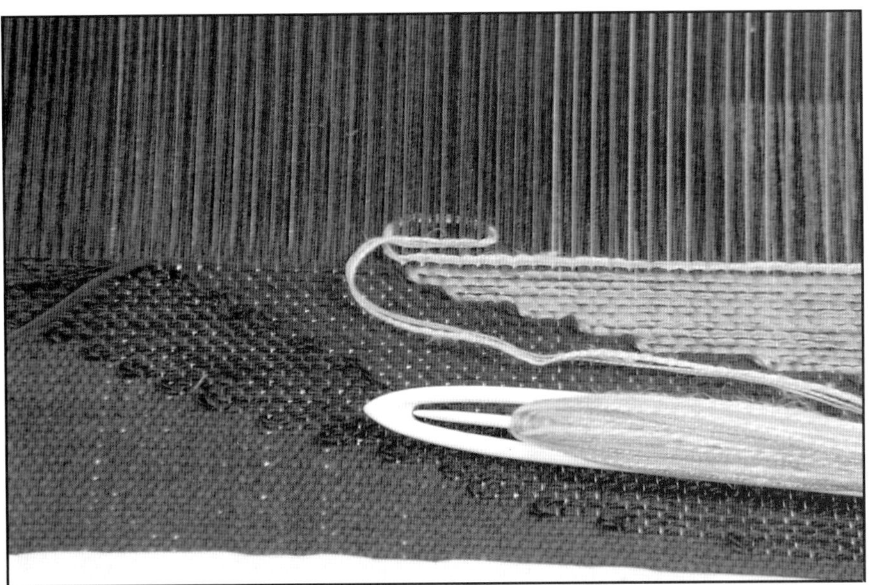

All the shuttles do not need to go in the same direction all the time. On a diagonal or a curve it is sometimes better if they reverse directions as shown in this photograph.

row back because the tie-downs become an integral part of the fabric. If the error is farther back, you must unweave.

Shuttle going the wrong direction

If you realize that the shuttles are out of sequence, it is best to stop and find the error. If you have simply omitted a row of pattern weft, you can restore the weaving order by laying in an extra pattern weft. Since your ground weft is already in place, lift shaft 3 or 4 (depending on the sequence), lay in the extra pattern weft and beat.

Sometimes you will not see that you have left out a sequence of pattern weft until you have taken your fabric from the loom. It is possible to needle-weave in additional pattern inlay yarn. However, this type of repair work is limited because it is very difficult to raise tie-downs after they have become an integral part of the background cloth.

You can change the direction of a shuttle by opening the ground shed for the next pick, placing the shuttle in the ground behind the design you are weaving and coming up where you want to be. Beat. Then inlay under the appropriate tie-down warps followed by ground weft in the ground shed. The weft in the tie-down shed will cover the "tunnel through" yarn in the ground shed.

Conclusion

The Theo Moorman weave is not difficult. With the techniques described here and attention to the aspects of good design described in the preceding chapters, it is possible to produce striking pictorial weaving in wall hangings, table runners, pillows, clothing, and rugs. To these uses we turn in the next chapters.

Weave-Play Exercise

Writers do free-association timed writings to warm up for writing or loosen up their style. A similar exercise is available to weavers using the Moorman technique. This exercise will help you discover your ability to "design" at the loom as you weave.
Beware: you may become so enamored with this "composing with objects" that pattern weaving will become a thing of the past!
For more discussion of using unusual materials, see chapter 11, Gateways.

Steps

1. Add 12 to 18 inches to the length of a current warp you are preparing to wind for another exercise in this book or to a Moorman project you have already planned. For this exercise the color or the material of the ground warp and weft is not crucial.
2. Once the other exercise or project is complete, weave two inches of plain weave to start your weave-play exercise.
3. Walk around your studio, house, garage, yard, or neighborhood and collect objects. The items you gather can be related or in contrast to each other. The examples on the next page use feathers, mesh bags, a rock, grosgrain ribbon, grass, seed pods, stem with leaves, sewing braid and sewing trim, leaves, handmade paper, party spangles, shoestring, and beads. More examples of weave-play are included on the CD-ROM.
4. If you want the inlaid objects to be prominent, wind a shuttle of ground weft to match the ground warp. If you want to play with different ground wefts, you can add another point of interest to the weaving.
5. Lay out all the materials you gathered next to the loom. Start weaving and randomly choosing objects to inlay. You may find you'll use just a few of the items or all of them. You may want to leave a lot of space between each inlaid item or you may completely cover the surface of the ground.
6. If you are using objects from nature, consider inlaying a stick from a tree branch, bamboo, or bone at the beginning/ending or both of the weave-play exercise. Then the sample can be hung easily.
7. If you are inlaying a lot of bulky items, the length of your weaving will be limited by the distance from your reed, to the breast beam, to the cloth beam. You need to cut off the weaving before it rolls around the cloth beam.

Inlaying Tips

A) *Bulky three-dimensional objects (un-drillable)*
You will need to wrap rocks, shells, large beads, coins, jewelry, clay, glass fragments, and so forth before inlaying. Use wire, monofilament, thread, or yarn to wrap the object. Leave a tail at least six inches long on each end of the wrapping. Inlay the tail of the wrapping material and allow the object to sit freely on the surface of the weaving.

B) *Bulky three-dimensional objects (drillable)*
Drill a small hole in the object and string it on a wire, monofilament, thread or yarn. Then continue as in the previous paragraph.

C) *Sticks, grass, pine needles, feathers, flowers, leaves, herbs, hair, fleece, paper, wire, ribbon, and so forth*
You can inlay single items, or a bunch of them, in one inlay shed. The entire length of the object can be placed in the inlay shed, or part of the object can be inlaid in the shed while the rest of the object sits freely on the surface of the weaving. Flexible objects like ribbon and wire can be wrapped around individual tie-down warps, then travel through the inlay shed to the next area of wrapping. The loops will stay on the surface of the weaving and not be crushed when beating in the ground weft.

D) *Inlaid objects that are larger in diameter than the ground weft*
These items are inlaid in one of the tie-down sheds. While keeping this tie-down shaft raised, weave a number of ground picks underneath the object to build up a solid ground beneath it. Here's how:
Inlay the object with shaft 3 or shaft 4 raised. For the rest of these directions, assume that you have just inlaid with shaft 3 raised.
Throw a ground weft in 1-3.
Keep shaft 3 raised, add 2-4 and throw the ground weft.

Throw ground weft again in 1-3.

Keep shaft 3 raised, add 2-4 and throw the ground weft.

Continue this sequence until ground weft is packed underneath the bulky object.

When shaft 3 is finally lowered, the tie-down warps of shaft 3 will have a long float, but if the object is at least three inches long, it will stay in place in the weaving and the ground fabric will not be distorted.

E) Beads and buttons

String the beads or buttons on thread, monofilament, wire, or yarn. Leave enough thread so the items can be slid around and used in a number of rows.

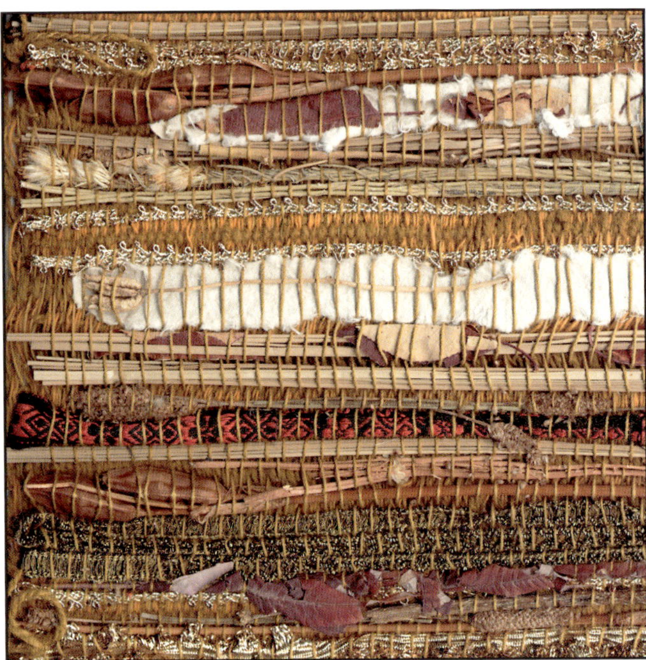

Examples of Weave-Play Exercises

(upper left) **This weave-play exercise was done on a double warp overlay warp so it is weft-faced. I left space between objects to uncrowd the composition. NS**

(upper right) **This weave-play was done on an opaque warp. I inlaid objects in almost every row to create a solid textural explosion. NS**

(lower left) **This example of weave-play was done by a student at Fiber Arts School in La Habra, CA.**

CHAPTER 7

Pictorial Weaving

THEO MOORMAN'S WORK focused on her wall hangings. Her later years were spent using her weaving and artistic experience to express ideas about nature, but she also continued to explore the structure of the weave that is named for her. When Peter Collingwood interviewed her for Handwoven in 1988, she confided that the desire to create a picture and the desire to investigate the weave structure were often at odds with one another.

Rock formations and sculptural forms inspired Theo. Drawing abstract shapes was often frustrating, but then translating these rough sketches into pictorial weavings and choosing materials to express the essence of the objects delighted her. She wove many small-scale hangings, which she sold when she taught around the world.

DARK FORM 12″ x 10″
A Theo Moorman weaving from the collection of Eileen Chadwick.

The direction you choose to work pictorially will be as individual as that of the painter on canvas.

COME TO THE CROSS 3′ x 12′ with angular top
This piece was commissioned for the chapel of the Northfield (MN) Retirement Center to honor a retiring CEO. The cross is centered in the yellow area representing the light radiating from the cross. The ground fabric is entirely covered by the weft yarns forming the design. JH

Some will focus on color; others, on shape and texture; and others, on the composition and perspective. Whether you are creating a richly detailed wall hanging, whimsical pillows, paraments for the church, decorative table linens, or striking rugs, the full potential of the Moorman technique is realized in pictorial weaving.

When weavers first try this technique, they comment on the tapestry-like effects easily achieved by this structure. Theo herself described it as a "poor man's tapestry." While the visual effect can be similar, the structure is different. Traditional tapestry is a single layer composed of discontinuous wefts. The Moorman weave produces two layers. It is technically a plain weave derivative with overlay or supplemental brocade. The pattern inlay yarns lie on top of the ground. The weaver chooses to cover the ground with pattern inlay yarn as a painter saturates the canvas; or the weaver allows the ground to serve as a surface for the placement of individual motifs that allow the ground to show through, as you would decorate a cake.

I interviewed weavers for the original book, *Weaving That Sings*. When they were asked why they used the Moorman technique for pictorial weaving, the overwhelming consensus was that it was faster than traditional tapestry. Another frequently mentioned consideration was that it was easier to achieve a painterly effect—especially if one was emulating Impressionism. Some weavers liked the flexibility to adjust design and materials as they wove. Not all of the weavers used full-sized cartoons; some wove from sketches and changed the design as they proceeded. Others noted lightness of the finished fabric and freedom of movement in the design as desirable factors. A few weavers mentioned that a modest amount of specialty yarn could be used quite effectively and the fact that the firm ground fabric is also an excellent base for stitchery, embroidery, or other surface design.

Weavers who want to push the Moorman technique to appear three-dimensional have experimented with overlapping design areas, inserted additional design weft into the ground fabric, and used unspun roving for pattern weft. The wide variety of responses from artists working with the Theo Moorman technique underscores the continuing appeal of this structure as a way to create pictorial pieces and as an area for weaverly exploration.

The wall hangings, pillow, and liturgical work included in this chapter all use a sett of 24 e.p.i.—16 ground and 8 tie-down warps. See the Opaque Draft on page19 in chapter 3.

Designing a wall hanging

Designing any form of weaving requires an understanding of the function of the piece and the structure of the weave you are using. Here are some questions to be considered when designing wall hangings.

Where will the piece hang?

For a weaving you create for yourself, you probably have a place in mind to hang it before you weave it. Commission work or hangings given as gifts may have more stipulations to consider:

- The color tones of the surrounding area
- The dimensions of the hanging relative to the surrounding area
- Architectural elements such as shelves, windows, ceiling height, door frames
- Other artwork
- Competing textiles such as drapes, upholstery, throws
- Decorating style
- Floor covering, rugs, wallpaper, furniture
- Switches and thermostats on the walls
- The type of light. Whether the light source is incandescent, fluorescent, full spectrum, or natural will affect the tone and durability of the colors in your yarn.

Will the piece hang vertically or horizontally?

Some weavings can be woven the same direction they will hang. But other designs need to be turned ninety degrees from the direction they will hang in order to fit on the loom. Certain shapes and motifs weave better from one direction (the design edges are more precise). So thinking during the designing process about the direction your weaving will hang can very much affect the look of the woven piece. Another consideration in weaving a piece vertically and then hanging it horizontally is the need for a hem. Leave three inches of plain weave that has no pattern inlay at each edge of the weaving. These edges will then become the top and bottom of the weaving when it is hung; they will be pressed into a hem. The weight of the hem will help the weaving hang better.

What kind of device will hold the piece? Will this device show or be hidden?

Correct mounting enhances the presentation of a piece just as incorrect or careless mounting will detract from it. A hanging device can be functional, decorative, or part of the design. Functional devices include:

- A sleeve for a rod to slide through
- A board with a Velcro strip matched by a strip on the wall hanging
- Any variety of quilt-hanging devices
- A foamcore backing
- A picture frame.

Decorative hangers need to be considered during the design process so the color and ornamentation of the device don't compete with the woven piece. Stitchery shops carry metal and wooden decorative hangers for cross-stitch, needlepoint, and other handwork. Woodcarvers and blacksmiths can be found all across the country; a custom-made hanging device carved or forged specifically for your design would be a lovely collaboration. For a weaver who marries the hanging device and the weaving, see Peter Horsfall's work in chapter 11.

Will it be viewed from a distance, close up, or both?

The Moorman weave can be appreciated from a distance because it effectively translates bold simple shapes to the fabric. From a distance the eye fills in the jagged edges of pattern inlay of curved shapes. In large pieces, the interplay of positive and negative space assumes great importance. The design on a small weaving in your bathroom will be scrutinized much more closely than a hanging at the front of a church. For a weaving to be viewed up close, using finer pattern inlay yarns and taking more care at the edges of the shape can create smoother design edges. The ground fabric and the pattern inlay interact with each other more intimately in designs that will be seen at close range. You could consider designing in the ground layer also. Inlaying discontinuous weft along with the ground weft creates a more complex background. If you have more than four shafts, using a ground structure like a twill or block structure adds a background pattern. For examples of combining more complex weave structures with fine tie-down warp, see chapter 11.

Design focus

Whether you are creating wall hangings, liturgical weavings, pillows, table linens, or rugs there are more general questions to recognize.

What will be the focal point?

If you are clear about what you want to express in your pictorial weaving, the final product will be stronger. Many weavers just start with some yarns they like and figure out what to do with them. By this point you know that this weave structure is controlled by you and not by the loom. I often write about a piece I am planning before I start the design process. This exercise helps me clarify what I am weaving and why I am weaving it. My focus may change as I design, but at least I have a clear starting point from which to proceed. Sharing your design ideas with fellow weavers or other artists can provide valuable feedback before you take it to the loom.

What yarn will be appropriate for this piece?

Since this weave allows nearly total saturation of color in the pattern weft, yarn color is an important factor in the design process. Textured yarns can overpower the design in a small wall hanging, or the textured material can become the focus of a design.

Design tricks

Several design tricks are particularly useful and easy to render in the Theo Moorman technique. Some of these may help you express your ideas or themes in pictorial hangings.

Woven Words—Words can be used alone or with other design motifs in the Moorman weave. Letters can be hand drawn or printed from a computer and stylized to fit the weaving.

Positive and Negative Space—With an opaque ground fabric, it is possible to form shapes or letters in both positive and negative shapes—that is, the shapes can be formed by the pattern weft on the background or they can be outlined by the pattern weft.

Tessellation—The renowned artist, M.C. Escher, is known for his designs that use tessellation—that is, where one motif repeated over and over gradually transforms into a different motif as the spacing between motifs changes. Simple forms of tessellation can be achieved in the Theo Moorman technique. There are several excellent websites that show examples of tessellation and give assistance in designing your own tessellating designs. See Resources.

Certain objects or projects, besides wall hangings, are particularly good places to experiment

text continues on page 50

Memories Triptych *each 24″ x 24″*
The Pansy Patch. *(left)* **My Dad would plant a patch of pansies each spring; it was fun to check out the new colors and look into the faces of those lovely flowers.**
Three Sisters, One Bicycle. *(center)* **Three sisters meant lots of sharing, but when our only new bicycle arrived on my birthday, sharing became a difficult task.**
Catching Butterflies. *(right)* **Many happy hours were spent catching butterflies. Finding a new species, adding to my extensive collection, and studying about them led to an award for a summer camping experience.** JH

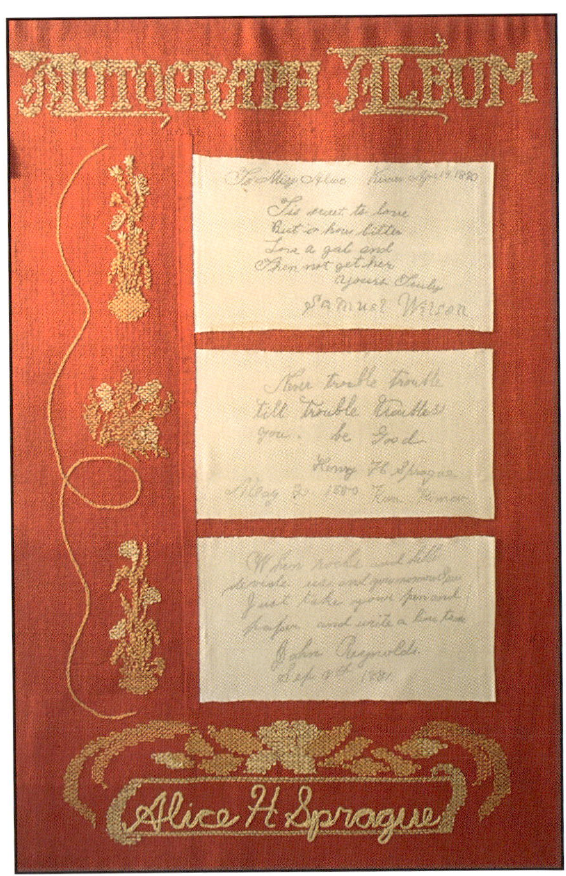

Autograph Album: Pages from the past 24″ x 36″
I discovered my grandmother's childhood autograph album in a family collection of memorabilia. Recording some of the verses and designs from the precious little red book led to a new avenue of weaving very fine cotton cloth to print upon. I then combined the printed fabric with my love of the Theo Moorman technique for the pictorial background. JH

Normandale Lutheran Church, Edina, Minnesota 12″ x 108″
A set of altar panels and pastoral stoles for the green seasons of the church year were designed to complement a new altar and pulpit. JH

Banner 4′ x 8′ and detail
These banners are the backdrop for Nadine's musical group, Straw Into Gold. The letters are inlaid as positive shapes. The wheat creates an organic texture.

with the pictorial capabilities of the Theo Moorman technique.

Pillows and table linens

The Moorman weave works well in these small formats. A pillow would be an excellent place to try out a design for a larger rug or wall hanging. The back of the pillow can have additional pattern inlay, be plain weave, or use commercial fabric. Since plates and serving ware often cover up much of a placemat or table runner, concentrating the design around the outside edges will show off more of the design.

Liturgical weaving

Christian church denominations that follow the seasons of the liturgical year use cloth as part of the ritual of celebration. Easter, Pentecost, Ordinary Time, Advent, Christmas, Epiphany, and Lent have colors and symbols associated with them. These symbols and colors lend themselves well to interpretation in the Moorman weave. The range of work found in Christian churches includes: stoles, chasubles, copes, miters, and dalmatics for ministers, priests, and deacons; altar and table coverings; veil and burse; pulpit hangings; baptismal hangings; funeral palls; and wall hangings. Special consideration must be taken to choose materials and finishing techniques that will hold up well since these weavings will be used for many years.

In the Jewish tradition, the tallit (prayer shawl), kippah (skullcap), and bag to hold them are an important part of synagogue services, holy days and Bar/Bat Mitzvahs. Challah covers, Passover textiles, chuppahs, torah covers, and ark curtains are also cloth objects important to the tradition. Moorman techniques are sometimes used in Judaic textiles. A thorough examination of liturgical weavings and their history and design can be found in *Weaving for Worship: Handweaving for Churches and Synagogues* by Joyce Harter and Lucy Brusic.

Rugs

The versatile four-shaft Moorman weave can be used in rugs. The joy is a rug that moves away from the grid structure and has pictorial possibilities. If rugs are going to be walked on, a few changes in materials and sett should be considered. A 20/2 tie-down warp will wear very quickly. A 10/2 cotton tie-down is a better choice for a well-trampled rug. Ground warp could be 3/2 cotton or carpet warp but I like using 12/6 cotton seine twine. I've changed the sett to 20 e.p.i. with 10 ground warps and 10 tie-down warps in a 10-dent reed. The close sett of the tie-downs holds the pattern inlay yarns securely so passing feet won't pull them out. Chapter 10 also includes rugs but in the double warp overlay technique, which is a Peter Collingwood three-end unit structure combined with the Theo Moorman technique. These double warp overlay rugs require six shafts and are reversible. The two rugs pictured on p. 53 were woven on four shafts following the draft at the end of this chapter.

Limitations of the Theo Moorman technique

Although this weave structure offers flexibility and freedom, it won't do it all! In most cases it is faster than traditional tapestry, but if you use fine yarns or develop a design that covers the entire surface, you may find that a work in the Moorman technique takes as long as traditional tapestry. The finer the sett of the fabric, the longer the set-up time will be. Because you are winding and warping two warps, extra time and care must be taken to achieve error-free threading and equal tension.

If great detail is your goal, then this technique may not work for you. The distance between tie-down threads determines the type of line that can be achieved. For example, a circular shape viewed close up will have jagged edges. When viewed at a distance, the eye will see a truer circle. Fine detail can be added with hand or machine stitching after the piece has been woven.

The weave structure named for Theo Moorman continues to fascinate and intrigue weavers just as it fascinated and challenged her. Many possibilities lie hidden within the structure, and it may be overwhelming to deal with them all. It will help to focus on one or two aspects of the weave until you find the parts that intrigue you. If one aspect does not satisfy you, look to another. You may not continue to work with this structure for the rest of your life, but it contains a lifetime of possibilities and challenges.

Opaque Draft for Four-Shaft Rugs

						X						X					
			X						X						X		
		O			O			O			O			O			O
*	O			O			O			O			O			O	

		■	■
■	■		
			■
■			

Plain weave

X			
			X
X			
			X
	P		
G			
		P	
			G
	P		
G			
		P	
			G

There are errors in this draft. Please print the CORRECTED draft, *Opaque Draft for Four-Shaft Rugs* from Chapter Seven on the CD-ROM version 2.1 and higher.

Treadling: same as Opaque Draft

Tie-up: same as Opaque Draft

Ends per inch: 20

Ground: 10 ends, equivalent of 12/6 cotton seine twine = X

Tie-Down: 10 ends, 10/2 cotton = O

Reed: 10 dent, sleying order as follows:

2 ends per dent: one ground, one tie-down (one X and one O)

*The half-moon shapes underneath the threading chart show ends sleyed through one dent in the reed.

Selvage—Chose the rug selvage you like:

Add a floating supplementary selvage on each edge

OR wind three extra ground warps for each edge. Thread all three through the same heddle and sley all three through the same dent in the reed.

Weft: G= ground weft heavier than ground warp. Wool or cotton yarn or fabric strips.

P= pattern weft in various weights and textures

Note: In this project as in all other instructions in this book, the right-hand side of the warp is determined by the position of the weaver sitting at the loom. That is, the right side of the warp is at your right hand when you are facing the front beam of the loom.

A Gallery of Pictorial Weaving

Orange Sun Pillow **10" x 11"**
This project was designed to teach all specific techniques used in the Theo Moorman weave—blocks, interrupt, crossover and weave-under. This project is included on the CD-ROM. JH

Celebration Stole. *(upper right)*
This stole uses all the colors of the church year. The cross is in the negative space created by inlaying around the edges of the cross form. The pastor wears this stole for holy days, weddings, baptisms, and other celebrations. NS

Advent Stole. *(lower right)*
This stole for a female clergy emphasizes the story of Elizabeth and Mary. NS

KEYSTONE BLUES 3′ x 5′

Keystone Blues *(left)* **was woven on four shafts. The spiral design represents the never-ending life cycle on a farm. Denim strips of overalls from Nadine, her father, and her grandfather were inlaid to create the spiral. Keystone was the name of an overall company.** NS

FOREST MOON WOMB 4′ x 6′ *(right)*

In this four-shaft rug, pattern inlay completely covers the ground. The image of a full moon shining down through a canopy of trees was the inspiration for this rug woven for a woman who lives on a tree farm. NS

Finishing touches for wall hangings

Needle-weave ends you have left when beginning or ending pattern weft yarns. These should be minimal if you have followed the directions about burying ends in the ground warp. The only weft yarns you should have to needle weave are those where a point began and those that occurred at the edge of the fabric.

When you have completed the needle-weaving, steam press your wall hanging on the back side. If this steaming is done on top of a heavy terry cloth towel, the pressing will enhance the texture of the weave. Hems can be steam-pressed and finished with a zig-zag stitch, a serger edge, or bound with tape.

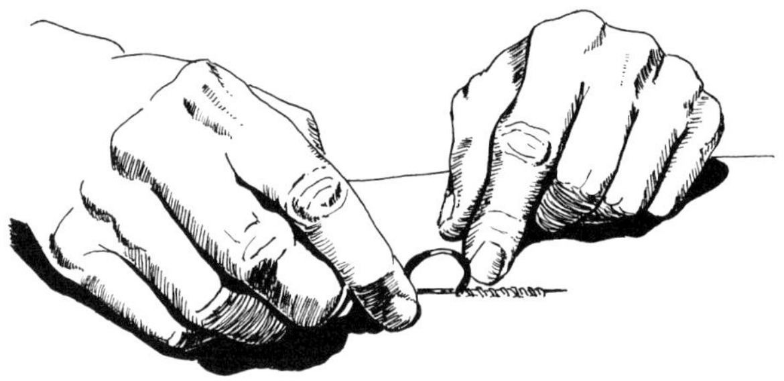

Needle-weave ends of yarn into your completed wall hanging.

Mounting a wall hanging

One way to mount a large hanging is to sew a casing made from commercial fabric to the top edge of the hanging. This casing makes a sleeve for a wooden slat. Put screw eyes in the slat, as shown, to attach to the wall. The weight of the hanging will be supported by the slat.

Another way to hang a piece is to use self-adhesive Velcro. Weave an extra three inches of plain weave along the top edge of the weaving. Sew the loop strip of one-inch wide Velcro onto the top edge of the reverse side of the weaving. Place the hook strip of self-adhesive Velcro on a piece of wood two inches down from the top edge on the back side. This construction allows the woven

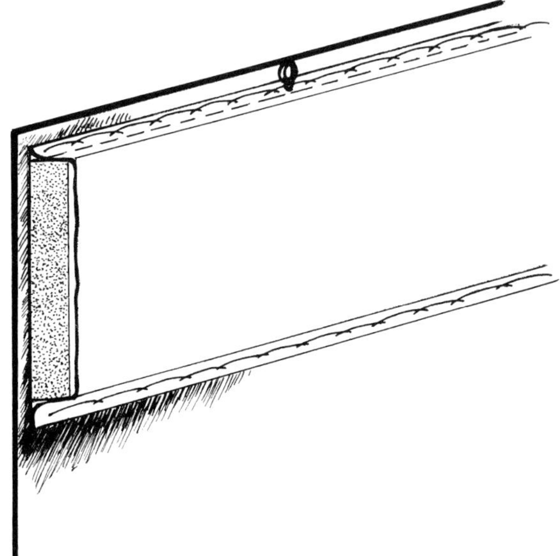

One way to hang a piece: a fabric casing is sewed to the back of the completed wall hanging.

hanging to go up and over the wood and hang down freely. Screw the wood strip to the wall underneath the hanging.

There are also commercial hanging devices for textiles available if all you want to do is purchase and hang with no sewing or gluing. One such device is DisplayAway. (See Resources.)

Another hanging method: use Velcro strips.

Mounting on foamcore

Another form of mounting can be done by using archival ¼-inch foamcore board, linen tape or archival double-stick tape, and a macramé braid for edging and hanging loops. Yarns used in the weaving project will make a coordinated edging, and the textural surface of your weaving will be enhanced.

The weaving needs to have two inches of plain weave all around. The plain weave will be taped to the back of the foamcore board.

Cut a piece of archival foamcore board the exact size of the weaving. Fasten the two inches of plain weave to the back of the board with archival double-stick tape. This tape can be used on all four edges.

Use the same technique that painters use to mount canvas on a stretcher. Affix the corners first, then work from the middle of a side out to each corner. Miter the extra material on the corners, smoothing the fabric on all of the edges so that only the designed woven surface remains on the front. The extra border material on the back is now ready for the linen tape.

Using one-inch linen tape, cut the desired amount to cover all of the edges and apply. If yarns of the weaving are fuzzy or the tape isn't sticking to the fabric, try spraying the edges of the fabric with starch. Allow the starch to dry before applying the tape.

Double half-hitch braid

To make a double half-hitch braid for the border, measure several strands of yarn (two, four, or six) at least three times the length needed to circumnavigate your work.

Cut the strands of yarn in half and wind each group onto a netting shuttle. You will have two netting shuttles. It may seem that you have a lot of yarn but this ratio will give you the correct amount when you are done knotting.

Place an overhand knot in all of the yarns. Pin the knot to a cork or foamcore board with a T-pin for security. Proceed to alternate tieing around each cord and pulling up tight. See Resources for websites on knotting. The alternating half-hitch produces a chainlike cord that is slightly stretchy. If you prefer a more solid braid, create a core with one or two yarns and braid around it.

This braid or cord can be sewn onto the mounted piece all around the edge with a matching strong thread, such as button thread, by sewing through the braid with small stitches.

A cover for the back of your work can be a plain muslin fabric or some coordinating fabric, which can be sewn to the woven fabric stretched over the edges of the foamcore. Loops of the braid can be sewn to the top for hanging if the project is less than 12 to 14 inches wide. Or a seine twine cord can be fastened to the two upper corners of a larger hanging, four inches down from the top on each side.

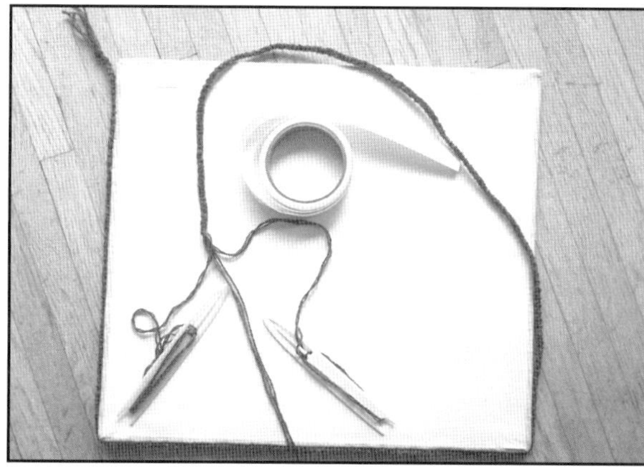

Muslin can be used for a backing over the foamcore board.

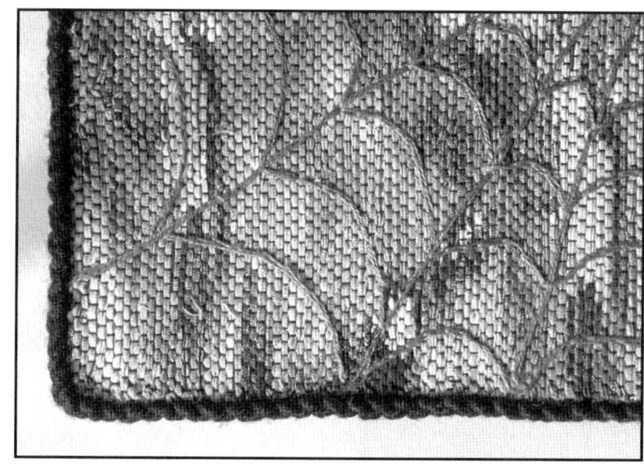

Half-hitch cord makes a good edge for a wall hanging.

Chapter 8

Multi-layered Inlay: Painting With Fabric Strips

A fabric store isn't the normal resource of weavers; most weavers think only of using fabric for rag rug weaving. Now, a new direction for the Theo Moorman weaving technique uses commercial fabric with the added inlay of yarns to create a design over strips of fabric. Joyce has developed a technique combining her love of fabric and continued fascination with the Moorman technique. We call it multi-layered inlay. With this new use for fabric, your quilt store may become your favorite weaving supplier. Joyce explains this new technique in the following pages.

Note that using fabric strips for pattern inlay in clothing and rugs and as upper ground and lower ground in double warp overlay projects is also discussed in chapters 9 and 10. The use of fabric in those chapters is different from the multi-layered inlay described here.

My love of commercial fabrics goes back many years, well before my weaving days began. Sewing for myself and my family was a necessity but I also enjoyed creating garments that would be worn and admired. Choosing the right fabric with the right design was exhilarating.

Now my interest in designing for the Moorman technique has taken a new direction. I use commercial fabrics as the inspiration for the pictorial design of wall hangings, pillows, and clothing. I was designing a vest with soft blue silk noil yarns when my eye caught a small piece of silk fabric with flying birds that would go well with it. I decided to try weaving the fabric in a block of strips on the front, hoping the birds would show up—but they were too small. Since my project was set for the Moorman technique, I simply inlaid some of the blue bird forms with yarn. The fabric strip was inlaid first, then the pattern yarn was placed on top of the surface of the fabric. That was my first lesson. I learned that it takes about three times as much fabric as surface to cover an area. Three inches of fabric weaves down to one inch in the woven piece.

Seagulls Vest

This long vest with pleats at the shoulder was woven in textured silk yarns to go with small pieces of silk fabric with bird motifs from a collection of Jack Lenor Larsen sample fabrics. This was the first time I wove fabric strips on the surface in the Moorman technique. When the birds did not show up on the woven piece, I used yarns as an overlay to form the bird shapes. JH

I purchased a Hoffman quilt fabric for my next project. This time I planned to line the vest fronts with the fabric and to use it in cut strips as a design element on the front panels as I was weaving. The fabric had subdued orange, green, and brown colors. Choosing yarns to complement the fabric for the body of the vest was important.

The flower form on the front of the Fall Colors vest seemed to go well with the wooden buttons that blended with the fabric.

The wonderful quilt fabrics on the market today are an inspiration in themselves. The batik fabrics, the tie-dyed fabrics, the subtle designs that look like sky or water; all of these have potential as background for a weaving in the Theo Moorman technique. The fabric is cut into narrow strips, ¼″ wide, and laid under the tie-down warps; a layer of yarn over them forms the design. Sometimes the fabric strips are laid in the sequence in which they have been cut; at other times combinations of different fabrics or coordinated fabrics are used. Yarn is thrown for the ground weft, completing the fabric and giving stability to the piece.

This use of fabric strips cut and used in sequence is similar to the "California Rags" work by Trudie Roberts: however, the use of the Theo Moorman threading with two sets of warp yarns takes the fabric strips in a different direction. As a painter of scenes lays a background color on a canvas and then begins to place the images he or she wants to show over that, you could think of this technique as painting with fabric: the fabrics are the background for a scene or a pictorial design.

Fall Colors Vest

This vest was inspired by the colors of the fabric that I used for the background inlay. A button competed the design. JH

Harvest Leaves Vest

The Harvest Leaves vest suggested another way to use the fabric strip weaving in the Theo Moorman technique. The yoke on the back and an area on the pockets are inlaid strips of the same fabric from which the reversible garment pieces are cut. JH

The process

Choose a distinctive fabric with an all-over design, one in which the colors saturate and are strong on the reverse side. Printed fabrics often do not have both sides of equal color. A fabric with circular movement or strong diagonals that move and give depth will make a fascinating background. Strong thrusts of color in bold shapes work well. Sample a few rows of your fabric strips to see the effect they will achieve before designing. For example, a strong-colored fabric may look very subdued when the strips are woven in place and may require stronger colors of yarns to achieve the desired design.

The steps

One sett for the warp is 24 e.p.i—16 ground and 8 tie-down warps. I have used other setts. For materials and sleying see the project at the end of this chapter.

1. Draw the design elements to accompany the commercial fabric design.

2. Prepare a cartoon with the design motifs you will inlay with yarn over the strips. A cartoon will assure your desired placement. See chapter 6 for cartoons. You can use a variety of warp and ground weft yarns, because they do not show. It is a way to use odd yarns that you do not want for other weavings.

3. Wash the fabric before cutting into strips.

4. Cut the fabric strips ¼″ wide on the straight grain. The strips need to be 2″ longer than the width of the finished weaving to allow for take-up. You need to leave 1″ hanging on the under side of each edge of the warp. For weavers unfamiliar with rotary cutting, Nancy Srebro-Johnson's *Rotary Magic* is a good reference.

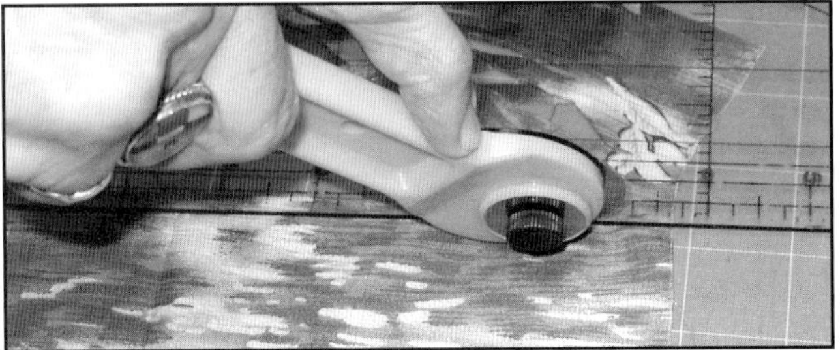

Cut the fabric strips with a rotary cutter.

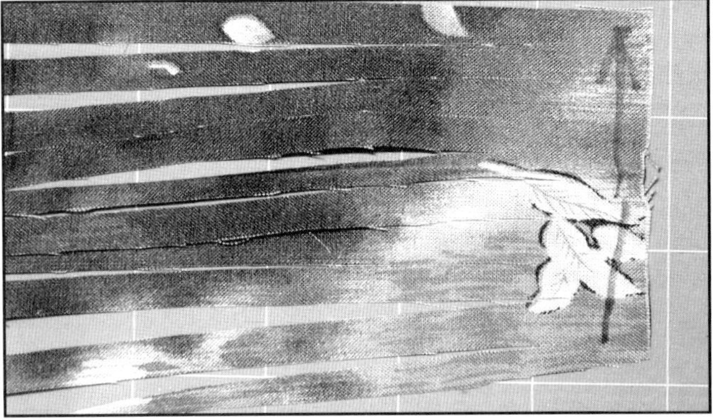

Mark one end of the fabric.

5. Cut three or four inches of fabric strips at a time with a rotary cutter on a self-healing mat. Don't cut all the way to the edge; leave ½″ inch uncut.

6. At one end of the uncut fabric draw an arrow with a felt tip marker. The point of the arrow is on the last strip.

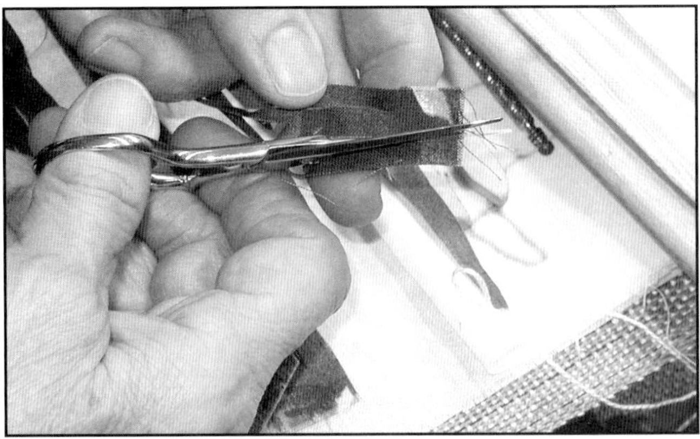

Cut the strips free as you weave.

7. As you weave at the loom, cut each strip of fabric free from the fabric section.

8. Raise the pattern inlay shed, either 3 or 4, and with a small empty wooden stick shuttle, scoot the strip across into place, with the fabric right side up.

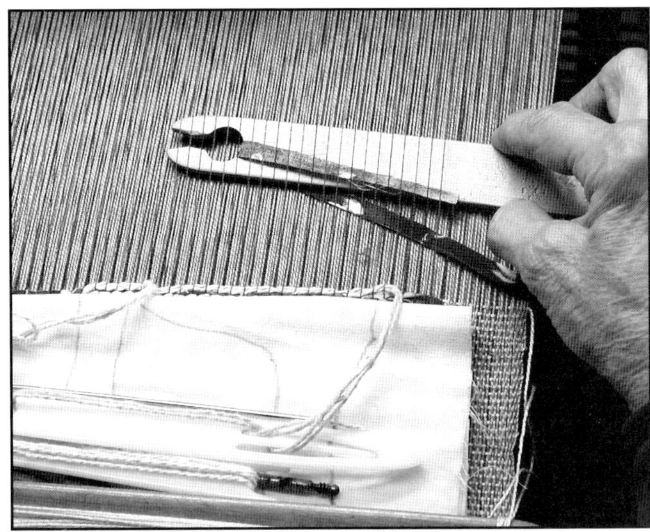

Use a small shuttle to scoot strip across warp.

9. Place the ends of the strip between two warp yarns on both edges of the weaving, leaving 1″ tails. Be sure to use the same two warp yarns each row. Try to keep the right side of the fabric up as the right side of the fabric has the more intense color.

Leave a tail of one inch at each edge of the weaving.

10. Then change to the ground shed, either 1-3 or 2-4. Beat fabric in place slowly with the ground shed open.

11. Now go back to the tie-down shed to place design yarns over the background fabric strip following the cartoon for the design element you wish to portray in this inlay technique. Design yarns are carried on netting shuttles.

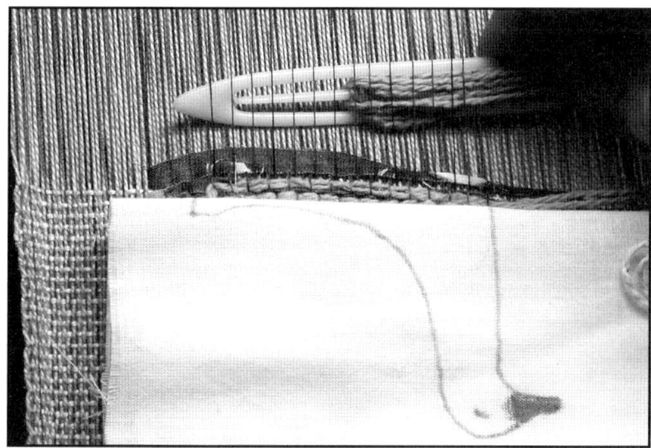

Design yarns are carried on netting shuttles.

A nut pick, a long tufting needle, or a small tapestry comb might be needed to help place the design yarn. Beat the pattern inlay yarn in place with the opposite tie-down shed open.

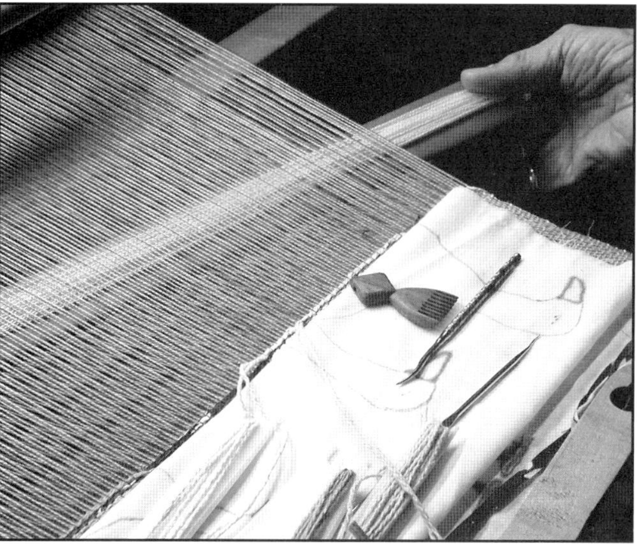

A nut pick and a small tapestry comb will be useful tools.

12. Next throw the ground weft (1-3 or 2-4) to lock all three layers in place. Ground weft can be carried on a stick shuttle or a large netting shuttle. Open the opposite ground shed and beat firmly.

Repeat this process and watch your image grow on the interesting background the fabric strips provide. Working with the Theo Moorman weave and commercial fabric is a wonderful way to challenge and develop your designing and weaving abilities.

The design process for multi-layered inlay can take two different approaches:

Design method A

Let the design of the fabric be a background for the design elements laid in on the surface. The wall hanging "Searching for the Spirit" is an example of this approach. The thrusts of color in the batik tie-dyed blue fabric are a beautiful background for a strong design woven in subtle colors. Several yarns were sampled before the soft multi-colored ribbon-like yarn was chosen.

SEARCHING FOR THE SPIRIT. 22″ x 31″
In this weaving the fabric is a background for the design. JH

Design method B

The other approach is to let the colors and the movement on the fabric suggest a design. The pillow, "Moon Prance Pillow" is an example of this. The strong brown, blue, green, and red swirling fabric seemed to suggest a design that would swirl around also. Using similar colors of yarns as the ground fabric gave the design the strength to complement the background of woven-in strips of cloth. Using the actual fabric as a backing for a pillow emphasizes the design elements.

This variation on the Moorman technique has some limitations. The design yarns that are laid in the shed with the fabric strips need to be firm enough or coarse enough to show up under the tie-down warps and on top of the fabric strips. The feel of the design will be casual—not so defined as a true tapestry. Moreover, these designs look better from a distance than they do close up.

Flight Pattern 31″ x 22″
A Hoffman quilt fabric that gave the impression of a sky became the background for an unusual verse. The doves were woven in to go with the saying. JH

MOON PRANCE PILLOW. 16″ x 16″
In this weaving the fabric suggested the design. JH

Exotic Flowers Pillow 16″ x 16″

This fabric needed to be sampled before the colors of yarns could be chosen. The sample determined the mute tones that the background would produce. JH

Seeing the Seaside 24″ x 32″

"Seeing the Seaside" took time to design. The strength of the striations on the batik tie-dyed fabric required that inlay yarns be doubled to be strong enough to be seen against the background of the fabric strips. I also needed a border to surround it. The choice of critters and shells cut from handwoven fabric and embroidered on the woven border was a challenge. JH

Website 12″x 12″

Website presented another way to use the fabric strips. The saying "Creative women have cobwebs in their corners, not in their minds" needed to have a cobweb embroidered on the surface beside the words. JH

Detail, Seeing the Seaside

Pillow in Multi-layered Inlay

Choosing a sett for multi-layered inlay depends on how much detail you have in your design. A chart of suggested setts can be found on page 107.

Warp calculation for a 12-dent reed:
288 ground warps
144 tie-down warps
Total ends: 432

Yarns and fabric for a 16″ x 16″ pillow

Ground warp: 5/2 perle cotton
Tie-down warp: 20/2 cotton
Ground weft: 5/2 perle cotton
Fabric strips: 1 yard of fabric. Cut back of pillow first, then make ¼-inch strips from the remaining fabric. Cut fabric strips 19 inches wide (2 inches wider than the warp.) One yard of fabric will be enough for pillows 16″ square. Fabric should be machine-washed before cutting.
Pattern weft: 3/2 perle cotton, thin ribbon-like yarns, or handspun yarns for second pattern weft to create designs.

Threading: Use standard Moorman threading: 1-2-3; 1-2-4. Repeat.

Sleying Sley 2 warps per dent in the following sequence:
*1 each of ground and tie-down, 1 each of ground and tie-down, 2 ground. (repeat from *) Width in reed: 17″.

Take-up and shrinkage: Allow 1″ extra in length when weaving; 16″ square requires 17″ of weaving.

Multi-layered inlay weaving sequence:

1. Raise shaft 3 and lay fabric strip under the tie-down warp; place end through to the back. Carry the fabric strip in the tie-down shed to one inch from the wedge of the warp. Place end of strip through to back. Raise 1-3 and beat.
2. Raise shaft 3 again and place design yarn over fabric strip following cartoon. Beat on opposite shed (4).
3. Raise shafts 1 and 3. Throw the ground weft shuttle the full width of the warp, close the shed, and beat.
4. Raise shaft 4. Lay the fabric strip under the tie-down yarn to fill the next row, close the shed, and beat. Raise shaft 4 again and place design yarn over fabric strip following the cartoon. Beat on opposite shed (3).
5. Raise shafts 2 and 4. Throw the ground weft shuttle, close the shed, and beat. You have two rows of pattern and two rows of ground cloth.

Finishing process

Steam press the reverse side of handwoven pillow block. Anchor the strips on the reverse side with a row of machine stitching. Fold back the woven ground fabric areas to expose just the cut strips. Make a fine machine stitch on the strips *only,* close to the woven edge, to secure them. Sew the pillow backing and the woven pillow block, right sides together. Leave an opening for stuffing in the pillow form. Make a closure with Velcro, a zipper, or buttons. For creative ideas for finishing pillows, see *Do It Yourself Fabric Décor.*

Chapter 9

Clothing: Garments in the Moorman Technique

Although Theo didn't envision using her technique for clothing, many weavers have adapted it for wearables. Vests, tops, sweaters, skirts, dresses, jackets, and coats can all be woven using the Theo Moorman technique. Moorman is well suited for clothing for many reasons.

The technique allows tapestry-like effects while maintaining a supple cloth that will drape; the weaver can produce clothing that is comfortable to wear. The garment will be one-of-a-kind.

Pattern inlay yarns show off because they sit on the surface; using small amounts of designer novelty yarns is like applying jewels. Designs are interesting from a distance; many handwoven garments lack luster from a distance because the design details are only visible at close range. Graphic, bold designs translate from paper to the garment without losing the energy of the design; the technique emphasizes the design rather than the fabric structure.

Choosing the garment design

The three-dimensional form of the human body presents design challenges very different from the flat surface of a wall hanging. The two avenues to clothing design are loom-shaped garments and tailored garments.

Loom-shaped garments

A sari is a loom-shaped garment draped to the body without cutting. Loom-shaped garments are simple to construct and sew. In addition, the simplicity of the garment allows you to emphasize design motifs and yarns that give color and texture. Inspiration can come from many sources. A resource file of clippings from magazines, photos, and postcards can help in the process. Dorothy Burnham's *Cut My Cote* is a fascinating introduction to ancient loom-shaped clothing and construction techniques. This inspirational resource would be an excellent way to begin the process of designing loom-shaped garments. Burnham points out that because the technology of weaving advanced faster than the technology of cutting and sewing, pre-industrial and ethnic garments were constructed to take advantage of selvages and straight edges.

Wherever you get your inspiration, simplify the design process by choosing one style, theme, or shape to emphasize in the garment form. Don't try to do everything at once.

Loom-shaped garments are not flattering on all body types. Loom-shaped garments can be modified by adding tucks or pleats and accessorized with belts, scarves, and large pins. At the end of this chapter, there is a pattern for a simple loom-shaped top that requires minimal sewing.

Tailored clothing

For weavers who are experienced sewers, making a tailored garment with handwoven cloth is a natural step. Weavers without sewing skills might consider weaving the cloth and then having a master clothier construct the garment.

Tailored garment forms can show off the assets of the body or flatteringly mask body parts. Another advantage of tailored garment forms is the availability of wonderful patterns. Besides the major commercial pattern companies like McCalls, Simplicity, Butterick, and Vogue, consider the American Kwik Sew, the British New Look, and the German Burda patterns.

There are currently many small independent pattern designers. An advantage of independent designers is that their patterns tend to be classic and timeless. The patterns stay in print and the designers keep adding to their collection. The big commercial companies change their patterns each season with the fashion industry. Many independent designers make patterns

text continues on page 66

Aquamarine Vest

This loom-shaped vest is woven in one piece. The same pattern was used for the Mondrian Vest on the next page. For vest pattern, see Resources. JH

Purple Tunic

This tunic illustrates a fine marriage of the Moorman technique with clothing. JH

AQUA DRESS AND JACKET

This ensemble was made from a Butterick pattern. Variegated silk yarns and wool/silk yarns were combined to test an idea Joyce had for a dress and jacket combining complementary design elements. Variegated yarns look striped when woven in long areas, but used in this zigzag design they don't appear as stripes. JH

MONDRIAN VEST

The design of the vest is unusual in that it was woven as one long piece of fabric with a square open area in the middle. When cut from the fabric, the two front pieces were exchanged so that the selvage edges became the front edges. The center back is pleated. JH

ZORRO COAT

This rust wool coat was a version of a Karen Noe Design jacket featured in the Swedish VAV Magazine. Joyce ordered the pattern but lengthened it into a coat. The coat is bound all around with handwoven fabric cut on the bias. The scarf is attached to the front closure of the coat. JH

that lend themselves to handwoven fabric and to designs rendered in the Moorman technique. See Resources for a list of independent pattern companies. Other possibilities with a tailored clothing form include shaping the bottom edges or bodice fronts to follow the inlaid pattern design.

FALL EQUINOX VEST

The bottom edge of the Fall Equinox vest reflects the shape of a maple leaf. NS

If you have a purchased garment that fits well and whose design you like, another possibility is to make a pattern from it. If you don't possess these skills, a professional pattern grader can do this for you.

I often start with a basic pattern that fits well and then make many different garments by modifying details.

Adding knitted cuffs, collar, sleeves or trim to tailored clothing is another way to create a unique garment.

For additional information on tailored clothing see *More On Moorman: Moorman Inlay Adapted to Clothing* by Heather Lyn Winslow.

PASSION CRONE
Passion Crone jacket was made from the pattern of a favorite jacket owned by a client. The front closure was changed and a pleat was added to the center back. NS

Designing the woven surface

Once you have decided on a garment shape, then you can decide how to create the fabric from which to make the garment.

Color

Take into account the colors that look good on the person for whom you are weaving the garment. Keep in mind the general rule that warm colors such as red, yellow, and orange will advance and appear larger, while cool colors such as blue and green will recede and minimize. If you are not comfortable using color, try planning a garment using neutrals. A field trip to a fine clothing retailer can help you refine color choices for your garment. I keep a file of color palettes from clothing catalogs for reference when choosing colors for my designs.

Unity of color is important in a garment. Generally the tie-down warp is chosen to blend with the ground warp. But contrasting colors are another option.

Yarns and materials

The Moorman weave allows you to use yarns ranging from fine silk to bulky wool, but determining the correct sett for the warp is crucial.

GRACE NOTES
This elegant jacket draws attention because of its lack of color. The simple design element was placed "gracefully" over the shoulder. A large flowered black silk fabric was the inspiration for this jacket. The silk fabric lines the front and becomes a shawl collar with the added touch of lined pockets. A twisted silk cording completes the jacket. JH

The beat for clothing should be much lighter than that for wall hangings. Experienced garment weavers stress the importance of sampling before beginning a garment. Sample yardage will allow you to determine the correct drape, weight, and "hand" for your garment design.

Quality fibers always enhance the appearance of a fabric. A good design capitalizes on the yarns to be used. In the ground warp I have had good success with fine yarns such as cotton, silk, silk/wool, wool, or wool/rayon combinations.

Aeron's Armor

The ground warp of this dress was wound in hand-dyed colors gradating from purple to red. The ground weft was space-dyed to bring out the saturation of the different color bands in the warp. The neckline of the dress was inlaid with a slubby multi-colored novelty knitting yarn. NS

Jaggerspun's Zephyr (50/50 silk wool) alternating with Jaggerspun's Heather (100% wool) is my favorite ground warp. For tie-downs I use fine cotton; a neutral gray will work with many different colors. Tie-down warps can range in size from serger thread to 8/2 DMC cotton. UKI makes 20/2 cotton in a wide range of colors and is my standard tie-down warp. Joyce likes 30/3 Gutermann silk sewing thread for clothing tie-down.

To reduce the bulk of the fabric, alternate single tie-down threads with doubled ground warps in a 12-dent reed. (For draft see page 76.) The fabric has only eighteen ends to the inch. To avoid long floats, you should have an interval of no more than one-quarter of an inch between the tie-down threads.

You can experiment with different setts to achieve different kinds of fabric. Here are some suggestions:

36 e.p.i. with 24 ground warps and 12 tie-downs

24 e.p.i. with 12 ground warps and 12 tie-downs

12 e.p.i. with 8 ground warps and 4 tie-downs.

The sett used for most garments in this chapter is 18 e.p.i. with 12 ground warps and 6 tie-downs.

Pattern areas are an excellent place to use exotic and specialty yarns such as mohair, angora, llama, alpaca, camel, and qivuit. This technique will show them off. Unique colors can be achieved by winding more than one yarn on the pattern weft shuttle. A variety of textured yarns on a single shuttle can also create interest. Because the tie-down warp is forgiving, a number of yarns can be wound together and packed in the pattern shed to achieve the desired saturation.

Because this weave allows pattern yarns to show fully, their properties are important. A smooth yarn will reflect light while a textured rough surface will appear darker.

The intended use of your garment will determine whether you want textured or smooth yarns on the surface. You would not, for example, want a textured yarn on the lower back of a coat where it might catch on furniture.

Because you often combine many different kinds of fiber in a Moorman garment, it is wise to weave a sample and finish it the way you expect to clean the garment. Washing, waulking (a fulling process), soaking, steaming, or dry-cleaning will each give a different hand to the fabric.

If the garment will be lined, consider the lining fabric before you weave the cloth. A lined garment may require a looser sett for the woven cloth, or a softer beat, than an unlined garment. Chose a lining material that will be compatible with the woven fabric. I line my garments woven with silk/wool yarns with a thin silk fabric. Rayon and cotton linings are also good choices for garment linings. When hand dyeing yarns for a garment, I often dye-paint the lining so the colors are compatible.

Very Berry Jacket.
Since the design on this jacket wraps around from the front to the bottom back edge, Joyce chose smooth pattern inlay yarns for the berry designs so they would not catch on furniture. JH

Lined garments can be made reversible. Reversible vests are great fun to weave and wear. Joyce has woven many vests where the design of the commercially printed lining fabric inspired the pattern inlay design on the reverse side. The lining fabric can also be cut on the bias and made into bias tape to bind the edges of the garment.

Planning the garment layout

As the shape of your garment and its design become more definite, the next step is to plan the layout. First remember to add length to the pattern pieces to allow for loom take-up and shrinkage in finishing. As a general rule of thumb, add one inch per foot to the pattern pieces. Add the length at the markings on commercial patterns where it says "shorten or lengthen here." If you are weaving with unfamiliar materials, sample first to see how much the fabric shrinks in length.

The width of your loom will be a deciding factor in planning garment layout. Loom-shaped garments can be made on narrow looms; panels can be sewn together. For tailored clothing lay out the pattern pieces on a squared cutting board as if you were ready to cut the pieces from fabric. This layout determines how wide and how long to make the warp.

Is your pattern inlay surface design going to be all over, or just on the bottom edge, or in the center back? If you plan your design to fit on a narrow panel, then you only have to weave a narrow strip with pattern inlay. The rest of the fabric for the garment can be woven on a separate, coordinating warp.

Panels woven using the Theo Moorman technique will hold up better in clothing if the warp is kept in a vertical position. However, there are some unique handwoven garment patterns for clothes cut on the bias. *Designer Diagonals* by Virginia West is a good place to start. Bias clothing with minimal Moorman inlay could be very interesting.

Whether loom-shaped or tailored garments are your choice, combining commercial fabric and panels of handwoven fabric is an excellent way

These reversible vests were featured in the article "Vest with a design edge" in Weavers', Spring 1998. One yard of commercial cloth with an interesting design element was the starting point. The vests were bound with bias binding cut from the commercial fabric.

Purple Swan Vest. (*top*) **The ground looks tweedy because of a threading sequence of different colored warp yarns. The design element is inspired by the commercial lining on the right.** JH

Red Buttons Vest. **A simple design element is repeated with color patches. When this vest was finished it seemed dull, so a collection of antique buttons added the finishing touch.** JH

FIDDLERS GREEN JACKET.
In Fiddlers Green the center back and center of each bodice pattern piece were modified to insert a design panel. The green inlay panel was woven only seven inches wide. The red fabric for the rest of pattern pieces was warped in a Moorman fashion, (18 e.p.i.: 12 ground, 6 tie-down) but had no inlay placed in it. NS

to create a contemporary garment with minimal weaving time.

Pattern inlay design

Placement of the design on the garment is very important. Once I have a design motif I like, I draw the shape of the garment in a small scale and make multiple copies of this form. Then I experiment to decide how the motif will be placed on the garment. Once the design motif is placed, I make copies of the final design and try different color schemes by coloring with markers.

THAI JACKET
Joyce's Thai Jacket used a special fabric she was given as a gift by friends teaching in Jakarta, Indonesia. The inlay designs were inspired by the Thai fabric. The only handwoven fabric is in the right and left bodice pieces, where gold cotton yarns form the warp and weft. Joyce developed the jacket pattern from an original Thai jacket. For this jacket pattern, see Resources. JH

For a design that wraps around the body, I sew a full-sized muslin of the garment, and draw the design on the muslin to check that it flows and stops in the right places.

Utilizing the cartoon on the surface as described in chapter 6 will allow you to transfer your design motifs accurately to the weaving.

In the accompanying photos, the pattern inlay motif on the garments was inspired by the commercial cloth design used as lining or in combination with the woven fabric.

One Dozen Roses

A ziggy silk commercial lining with a border of white roses was the inspiration for this long jacket. The woven fabric was designed, and the rose motifs handwoven in the Theo Moorman technique, to go with the white border of the lining material. This white border became the shawl collar. JH

Guatemala Plus *(top)*

A treasured piece of fabric from Guatemala inspired this jacket. The design of the jacket required a mock-up of muslin fabric to be sure that the placement of the panels in the Theo Moorman technique complemented the design in the fabric. The designs on the handwoven panels reflect the design in the fabric. JH

Batik Reversible Vest *(bottom)*

The imported batik fabric of brown and blue swirls provided the design element for this reversible vest. The back is plain weave and the front sections are lined with the batik fabric. JH

After the weaving

There are many pitfalls in making handwoven clothing. Three that you can avoid are: improperly finishing the cloth when it comes off the loom, poor sewing in making up the garment, and forgetting to plan ahead for embellishments.

Finishing the fabric

You must do something to the cloth after taking it off the loom. Just what, varies depending on the materials used and the intended use of the garment. Here are some possibilities.

Washing

Serge the ends of the cloth. Fill a sink, tub, or washing machine with warm water. Add a mild, gentle soap like orvus paste. (Orvus paste is basically what most “quilt soaps” are. Save the money and go to the feed store. Orvus paste is sold in large containers for washing animals.) Place the fabric in the water and let it soak for an hour. Do not agitate the fabric. Drain out the water without rinsing the fabric; place the fabric in the spin cycle of a washing machine. Once the fabric is spun out, place it back in warm water to rinse. Swish it around a bit to make sure all the soap is out. Then spin it in the washing machine one more time. Allow the fabric to line dry. When dry or barely damp, steam press it on the wrong side. Pressing on the wrong side on top of a terry cloth towel will keep you from flattening out the pattern inlay yarns.

Hot or cold shrink

This method is a soapless way of washing cloth. Serge the ends of the woven fabric. Wrap your fabric, “jellyroll style,” in very damp sheeting and leave it overnight to relax the fibers. The sheeting can be either hot or cold depending on the fibers you are using. Unroll in the morning. Press the fabric on the wrong side on flannel sheets or terry cloth towels.

Steam pressing

If washing or hot/cold shrinking is too dramatic for the cloth (perhaps you are unsure of the color fastness of some of the yarns you used) then at the very least steam press the cloth. Anyone making clothing needs a professional steam iron. Professional steam irons differ from household irons in that they put out more steam with the rate controlled by the user. There are many brands on the market. I prefer the Sussman Pressmaster with a hanging water reservoir.

Sewing tips

Eventually, you will have to cut into your fabric to create your garment. Trace the outline of the clothing pattern pieces and the shapes of the inlay designs from the paper pattern onto clear 4mm plastic. If a pattern calls for ⅝″ seam allowances this is the place to reduce them to ⅜″ to avoid added bulk in the garment. The clear plastic allows you to line up the pattern piece exactly with the inlay design. Immediately after cutting, take the piece to the serger and serge around all cut edges.

Most garments need some interfacing in the neckline areas or center front. There are some excellent interfacings on the market today that work well in handwovens. Linda Kubik sells several different kinds of interfacing that work superbly with handwoven garments. See Resources.

If you don’t have the sewing skills to make a garment, have a professional sew it. Professional seamstresses know tricks for eliminating bulk in seams, getting collars and facings to lie correctly, and fitting garments to the human body. Having a professional sew will also solve the problem of cutting into your own cloth. I just cut away, but many weavers hate this part of making handwoven clothing.

Embellishment

Sometimes a garment can be beautifully woven and finished and still lack something. Embellishment may be the answer. Embellishment is an art in itself. Too much embellishment or thoughtless embellishment can be as bad as no embellishment at all. The more you create garments the more embellishment will play a role at the beginning of the design stage. Sometimes an entire garment can be inspired from a special button. Or the buttons may unite the pattern inlay and the garment design.

DETAIL OF HARVEST LEAVES VEST *(P. 51)*
The leaf buttons were added to the inlaid leaf shapes to accentuate the form. JH

DETAIL OF ONE DOZEN ROSES *(P. 72)*
Macramé braid can also be used for buttonhole loops. JH

Any closure on a jacket, vest, or dress can add a point of interest to a garment. Lois Ericson is the author of a number of books on inventive ideas for garment closures. Try starting with her *Opening and Closing*. Lois also designs patterns and writes books on innovative clothing.

If you own a fancy sewing machine, the array of embroidery designs you can achieve on these machines could be married to a Moorman garment. Hand embroidery is also a possibility. Ribbon embellishment and cardwoven trim can all enhance a garment and perhaps even inspire it.

Clothing is a personal statement and is as individual as its creator. If this chapter has caused you to stop and think before warping the loom for your next piece of clothing, whether in Moorman or some other technique, then reading this chapter has been time well spent. Take the time to plan the details. If you give your initial idea or spark the attention it deserves, you will be rewarded with a wonderful garment.

DETAIL OF BUTTON CLOSURE
Fall Colors vest *(p. 57)* JH

Project: Loom-shaped Square-Neck Top

RED SQUARES TOP
The simple inlaid rectangular shapes reflect the shape of the garment. Interest was added by using some variegated yarns for pattern inlay. The garment was woven with variegated silk noil and silk/wool yarns. This design has been published in weaving magazines over the years. The sleeves have been modified. JH

*The half moon shapes underneath the draft show the sleying order.

Ends per inch: 18 (12 ground warp and 6 tie-down)

Ground warp: Jaggerspun's Zephyr silk/wool and Heather 100% wool, wound together = 0.
(Or desired material equivalent to 10/2 cotton (silk, wool, linen, rayon, Tencel)

Tie-down warp: 20/2 cotton or equivalent in silk = X

Reed: 12-dent, alternate single tie-down warp with doubled ground warp

Ground weft: One strand of the group warp yarn or equivalent.

Pattern weft: Your choice, to suit the pattern inlay design

Picks per inch: Will vary depending on yarns used. Beat very gently to avoid packing.
A cloth that is very loose on the loom will finish nicely with washing.

Dimensions: 82″ x 27″ for size Small, Medium, or Large.

Total Warp Ends: 486
Ground: 324
Tie-Down: 162

Warp Length: 124″

Designing: Decide how long the sleeves of your top will be. Various design motifs, from simple to complicated, work well on this garment. Plan your design and colors; make a full-scale drawing of the design and then make a cartoon. See chapter 6, page 36.

Weaving:
Top Front:
Weave in header to allow warp to spread. Weave with sewing thread for one quarter of an inch to provide a secure edge for your garment. Weave 3″ of plain weave for a hem.

Sew the cartoon to the surface of the weaving to insure that the pattern inlay design is placed accurately. You may want to use a temple to maintain width as you weave. Weave 24″ while inlaying design for top front.

To create the square neck and the shoulder area:
At 24″ start using three shuttles for ground weft. Weave in from selvage 10½″ with shuttle #1. Weave the next 6″ with shuttle #2. Weave from this point to the other selvage with ground weft shuttle #3.

Weave with the three shuttles for 6″. You have created the front neck opening.

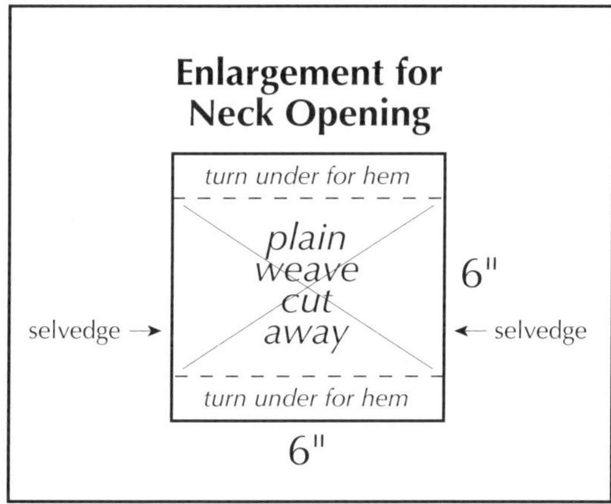

Top back:
After neck section is complete, go back to one ground shuttle. Continuing weaving the back of the top for another 24″. Weave 3″ of plain weave for hem.

Sleeves:
Continue weaving. Sew down cartoon if sleeves have pattern inlay design.

Short sleeves: Weave 6″ plus 3″ hem for each sleeve.

Long sleeves: Weave 16″ plus 3″ hem for each sleeve.

continued on next page

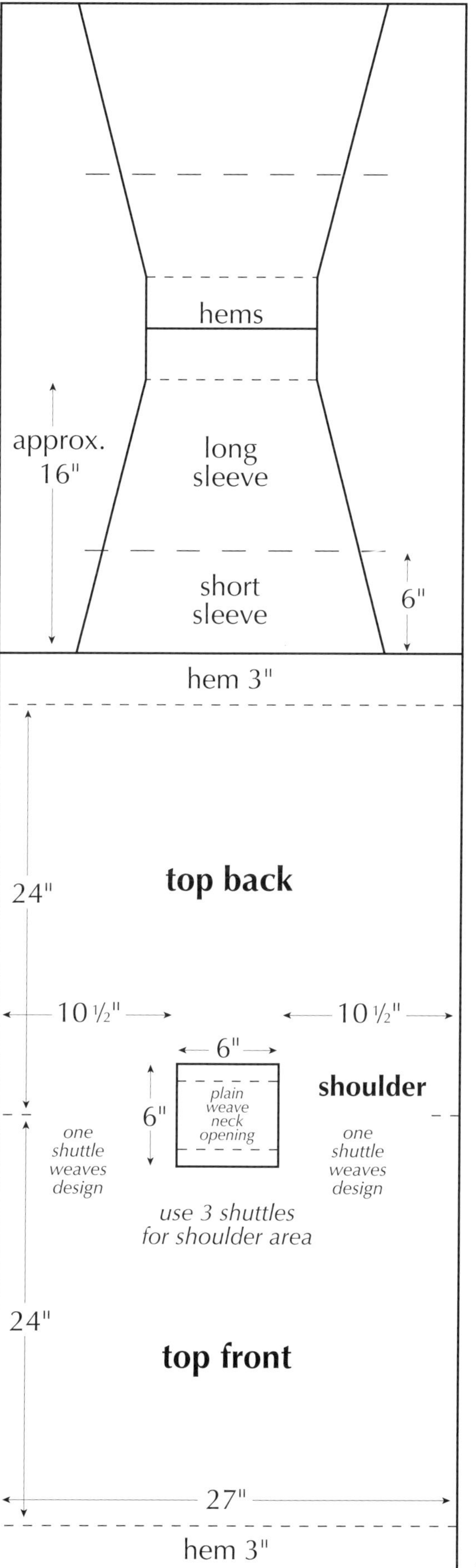

Finishing:
Serge ends of fabric. Soak fabric in warm water with gentle soap. Rinse. Line dry. Steam press from the wrong side.

Cut sleeve section of fabric apart from front and back section. Cut two sleeve shapes from the fabric.

Serge the bottom edges of the front and back pieces. You do not need to finish the selvage edges. Serge around all sides of the sleeve shape.

Each side of the neck edge is already finished as they are selvage edges created by weaving with three shuttles. Cut the 6″ of fabric in the neck opening in the middle at 3″. Serge the two cut edges.

Press these two flaps of fabric down to form the neck facing. With fusible web cut the same size as the neck facings, fuse the neck facing to the front and back of the top with a steam iron.

Pin the sleeves to either side of the top, matching the center of the sleeve with the center of the shoulder, as determined by measuring from the center of the neck opening. Sew sleeves in place with a ⅜″ seam.

Put the top front and back rights sides together. Pin in place. Starting at the bottom, sew ⅜″ side and underarm seam in one continuous seam. Repeat for the other side.

Hems:
Cut fusible web 3″ wide and the same circumference as the lower edge of the top. Press up a 3″ hem. Use a steam iron to fuse the hem in place with the fusible web. Do the same to hem the sleeves.

A Moorman Scarf

Black Magic Scarf 9″ x 72″
This scarf was woven on a spaced warp of black silk/wool with a black silk tie-down. The spaces in the warp were mirrored in the weft. The circles were inlaid in Moorman technique. The inlay yarn, which was rayon and silk, had been hand-dyed. The circles were designed to move through the spectrum as the scarf progressed. Design NS; Weaver JH

CHAPTER 10

Double Warp Overlay: Rugs and Table Runners

THEO MOORMAN NEVER used her technique for rugs or table runners. Her explorations took her in the direction of fine threads, wall hangings, and ways to make two-dimensional weaving appear to have three dimensions. But weavers wanting the freedom of flowing designs in rugs have adapted her weave.

A program by Barbara Hand at the Weavers Guild of Minnesota opened a way for Joyce to put bold, graphic designs on rugs and table runners.

Barbara Hand had combined the Theo Moorman technique with a Peter Collingwood three-end unit structure to create double warp overlay. Six shafts are required for this structure, which creates weft-faced weavings with two entirely different sides, and vertical channels which appear to run in a twill pattern. Joyce simplified Barbara Hand's tie-up, but most of the other draft information came from Hand's program and her article in Weavers' Journal, Spring 1983. Joyce added additional information on rugs in her article in Handwoven, November/December 1994. The table runner application is new in this book. A draft for both rugs and table runners is included at the end of this chapter.

HAPPY BIRTHDAY RUNNER
The words "Happy Birthday" stretch the full sixty inch length with a sunburst design awaiting the birthday cake. The underside in stripes of several blues can be used on other occasions. JH

Blue Boxes 33″ x 60″
This rug uses wool yarn for pattern inlay, upper ground and lower ground. The blue yarns were hand-dyed and used as a gradation on the underside of the rug. NS

This sample used several colors in the pattern weft. The ground weft was a fine neutral yarn in between the top and bottom layer. The heavy rug wools in the pattern weft made as close a turn-around as possible, sometimes utilizing shaft 6 at the beginning or ending of a block of color. JH

Preliminary advice

It is possible to weave a rug or table runner in the four-shaft Moorman technique detailed in chapter 7. However, the double warp overlay technique described in this chapter requires six shafts. It also requires a heavy floor loom. I weave on a forty-eight inch Macomber loom; for extra weight I have had several steel bars made by a welder. Each bar weighs twelve pounds. Holes in the bars allow me to attach them to the underside of the beater with long screws, washers, and wing nuts when I'm weaving rugs. It is best to consult your loom manufacturer before adding weight to get suggestions about the best place to attach weight to your loom and to find out how much weight the beater can bear.

Weaving with a temple will help keep the selvages of your rug from drawing in. In addition, if you have not had some experience with rug weaving or with the Theo Moorman technique, you may wish to begin by making a table runner or other small piece.

Design considerations

The upper surface of a rug or table runner in double warp overlay has great potential for masterful design. A good design will work from all angles. For rugs, a good design will invite people to walk on it. For table runners, the design will become the focal point of the table setting and will be readable from all sides of the table.

Design ideas can come from anywhere. Landscapes from National Geographic magazines or other travel magazines often contain pictures that can be translated into excellent designs. Scandinavian rya rugs are also a good source of inspiration. They combine circular shapes with rectangular forms. Two rug books I always turn to for design inspiration are *Weaving Contemporary Rag Rugs* and *Rug Weavers Source Book.*

Here are some design tips for double warp overlay rectangular rugs or table runners.

The tie-down warps are spaced farther apart in double warp overlay. Designs with fine detail should not be attempted.

Decide whether the pattern inlay design will completely cover the upper ground or if the upper ground will show through as a "canvas." This will help you determine what yarns to use for pattern inlay, upper ground, and lower ground.

Uneven areas of design are more attractive than even areas.

Rectangular shapes are more intriguing than square ones.

Diverse shapes are even more compelling.

Subtle variations in color will give simple designs a unique quality.

The rhythm established by repeating lines or patterns can lead the eye from one part of the design to another.

The back of the rug or table runner needs to be designed as well. The underside of the rug can contrast with or complement the front side.

Complementary materials and design

One advantage to a complementary underside is that sometimes yarns from the underside show through to the front side. If you are using the same yarns on the front and underside, this bleed-through is less likely to happen. If it does happen, then the underside yarns showing through to the top side are less noticeable when the yarns are the same size.

Weavers who like traditional weavings will appreciate the more formal look of rugs that use the same materials on the top and under sides.

By using the same materials on the front and back, the rug weft will pack better, creating a completely weft-faced sturdy rug.

Rugs using all wool, all cotton, or 100% any material, may clean more easily.

A stripe arrangement or a gradation of colors are two options for creating a complementary design.

Stripes

Don't overlook the design of stripes for the underside of the rug. Fabric companies like Pendleton Woolen Mills put much effort in designing stripes for each new line of fabric. The numbers from the Fibonacci series (each number is the sum of the preceding numbers—1, 1, 2, 3, 5, 8, 13, 21, 34 and so forth) can be used to find a pleasing arrangement of stripes for the back of the rug. For more information on the Fibonacci equations, see Resources. Other sources for arrangements of stripes include *Swedish Rag Rugs* and the *Rag Rug Handbook*.

Another possibility for the back of the rug is a color gradation. A color gradation can be achieved by dyeing yarns or purchasing yarns that move from dark to light in the same color tone or in analogous color tones. When changing from one yarn to another, blend the two yarns on the same shuttle for an inch or two before switching to the solid next color.

Contrasting materials and designs

Creating a weaving that makes a separate statement on each side is an amusing option in weaving with double warp overlay.

One side of the weaving can be woven for one holiday or event, while the other side is woven for a different holiday or event.

Using fabric strips (see chapter 8) on one side

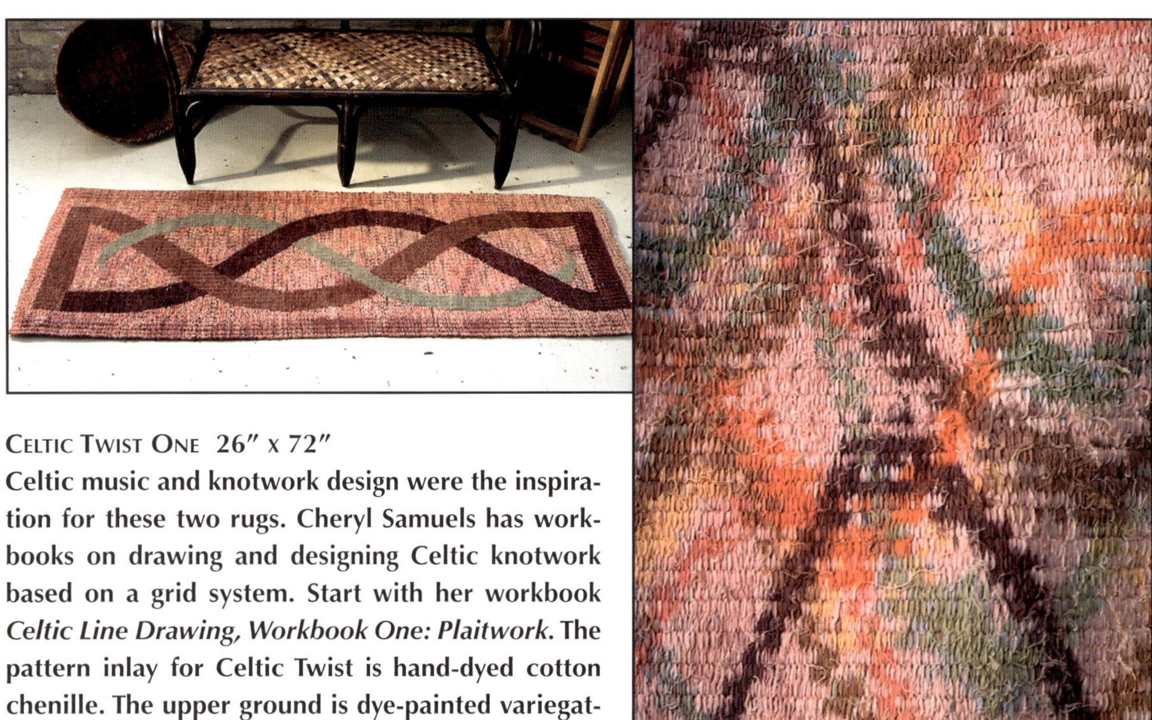

Celtic Twist One 26″ x 72″
Celtic music and knotwork design were the inspiration for these two rugs. Cheryl Samuels has workbooks on drawing and designing Celtic knotwork based on a grid system. Start with her workbook *Celtic Line Drawing, Workbook One: Plaitwork.* The pattern inlay for Celtic Twist is hand-dyed cotton chenille. The upper ground is dye-painted variegated cotton chenille. The lower ground is mock ikat dye-painted cotton fabric. NS

Celtic Twist Two 26″ x 72″
Celtic Twist Two was featured in Weavers,' Winter 1998. The pattern inlay is hand-dyed cotton chenille yarns. The upper ground is dye-painted variegated cotton chenille yarn and the lower ground is several different commercial drapery fabrics cut into 1/4-inch wide strips on the bias with two strips used together. Different fabrics were combined on the shuttle for a tweed-like effect. Design NS, Weaver JH

and yarns on the other will give the two sides two totally different looks.

However, using a combination of materials can make packing the weft tricky. Experimentation is required to find the correct number of weft yarns or width of material to use for the three layers (pattern inlay, upper ground, and lower ground) to achieve a completely weft-faced weaving.

Special design advice for rugs

The side of the rug that uses materials that are easy to clean may be the side to use "up" for everyday. The other side can be turned up for special occasions.

Using traditional wool yarns for one side and untraditional materials such as Polar Fleece for the other side will create one formal side and one informal side.

If you live with pets, children, or elderly people, consider the traffic the rug will get. Certain materials may hold up better with traffic. Use the sturdier material on the everyday side of the rug.

Transferring the design to the weaving

Use a cartoon as described in chapter 6. The color changes for the underside of the rug can be indicated on the cartoon by superimposing black lines across the cartoon to indicate where to change shuttles.

Remember to add length to the full-scale design before making the cartoon. Elongating the design and the rug to a 13-inch foot is adequate for most materials. This insures that the design won't squash down when you beat the rug.

Materials: Weft

Weft materials are many and varied. Successful wefts include 2- and 3-ply wool, rug wool, Matt Garn, handspun, commercially spun wool singles, Lopi knitting yarn, cotton chenille, and ¼-inch cotton, linen, or rayon fabric strips (cut either on the bias or across the selvage), Polar Fleece, cotton yarns, and rayon yarns. The bias cut fabric strips work better with double weave overlay because they have the "give" necessary for this weave.

For weavers who also enjoy dyeing materials for weaving, there are several possible weft ideas.

Ikat dyed yarn would also be striking for upper or lower ground weft in double warp overlay projects. Mary Zicafoose offers workshops in weft-faced ikat dyeing. See Resources.

Mock ikat dye-painted fabric

Several of the rugs featured in this chapter (see Springtime/Baby Blocks and Blue Intersections pages 94-95.) use mock ikat dye-painted fabric. Instructions for creating mock ikat dye-painted fabric are included at the end of this chapter.

Warp: Rugs

The most accommodating warp for this weave is 12/12 cotton seine twine for ground and 12/6 cotton seine twine for tie-down. See Resources. Other warp options are linen and wool.

Other possible warp materials are
- 8/5 linen for the ground and 8/2 linen for the tie-down or
- 4-ply worsted wool for the ground and 2-ply worsted wool for the tie-down.

Warp: Table runners

Joyce adapted double warp overlay to table runners. She uses 3/2 perle cotton ground warp and 8/2 cotton tie-down.

Rugs and table runners

In double warp overlay, each threading unit consists of three ground warp threads and three tie-down threads. There are the same number of tie-downs as there are warp threads. For rugs, at eight ends per inch, each unit of six threads will be three-quarters of an inch wide. For table runners, where you will use different yarns, the sett will be different, but the number of tie-downs will still equal the number of warp threads. To calculate how many units are needed, multiply the desired width of the rug or tablerunner by 4 and divide the result by 3. Add three extra ground warps at each selvage. For a warp calculation chart, see the double warp overlay draft on page 89.

Warp length

It is best to make a warp no longer than two or three yards for a double warp overlay project.

Dressing the loom

A second warp beam is a distinct advantage to allow for the differing take-up of the ground and tie-down threads in double warp overlay, especially for pieces wider than twenty-seven inches and longer than five feet. If you only have one beam, you should still wind two separate warp chains for the ground warp and tie-down warp. For further discussion of warping for the technique, see chapter 6.

Threading

The ground warp is placed on shafts 1-2-3.

The tie-down warp is threaded on shafts 4-5-6.

Thread in groups of twelve, alternating ground warp threads and tie-down threads:

Shaft 2 (ground)- shaft 5(tie-down)

Shaft 3 (ground)-shaft 6(tie-down)

Shaft1 (ground)-shaft 4(tie-down)

Selvages

At the selvage, the ground warp thread is tripled. The tripled warp threads are treated as a single thread in the heddles and the reed.

At the right selvage, thread the first three ground warp threads through one heddle, then thread a tie-down by itself.

Double the next two ground warps in one heddle, then continue alternating single ground warp and single tie-down.

Make a mirror image of this selvage at the left side, except that the very last thread on the left will be a tie-down on shaft 4.

To further clarify this threading, sit at the front of the loom. The right (tripled) selvage should be on shaft 2 and the left (tripled) selvage should be on shaft 1.

Sleying

Sley by twos into alternate dents, except at the selvage, where the three threads that have been put through the heddle together will also be sleyed together.

Tie-up

The following tie-up is the most practical way to keep your place while weaving. Strict adherence to the tie-up and the weaving sequence described below will minimize mistakes.

Starting from the left:

Tie shafts 1, 3, 4, and 6 to the first treadle.

Tie shafts 1 and 4 to the next treadle.

Tie shaft 4 to the third treadle.

Leave the fourth treadle empty.

Tie shaft 6 to the fifth treadle.

Leave the sixth treadle empty.

Tie shaft 5 to the seventh treadle.

Tie shafts 2 and 5 to the eighth treadle.

Tie shafts 2, 3, 5, and 6 to the ninth treadle.

The treadle tie-up for double warp overlay does not make a plain weave. For this purpose, tie up the two empty treadles (treadles four and six) to shafts 6-4-2 and 5-3-1. Weave a four-inch header at the beginning of the rug. Then untie the plain weave treadles to create spacers. Tie the plain weave treadles up again when you are ready to finish the rug with a header at the end.

Weaving order

The weaving order for double warp overlay has two sequences. For a table loom, copy the following chart and tape it to your loom. For a floor loom, simply follow the treadling sequence on the draft. Notice that you always start your shuttles on the side where your feet are treadling. Remember to leave a bubble or angle in the weft yarns to allow for take-up.

Weaving sequence chart

	Sequence A Lift Shafts	Sequence B Lift Shafts
Pattern weft	5	4
Upper ground	2-5	1-4
Lower ground	2-3-5-6	1-3-4-6

Beat all three at the same time.

Weaving tips

Before you begin to weave, spend some time trying different combinations of materials for the pattern weft as well as the upper ground and the lower ground. This sampling is especially important when you are using different materials in the upper ground from those you are using in the lower ground. For example, it may take three strands of cotton chenille yarn in the upper ground to cover an approximately ¼-inch strip of cloth used as lower ground weft. Sampling can be frustrating, but it will help you produce a flat, well-packed weaving where both the front and back surfaces are entirely weft-faced. Although the weight and thickness of the yarn in the upper ground and the lower ground should be nearly the same, the pattern weft can be of a different weight depending on the effect you desire—from transparent to opaque.

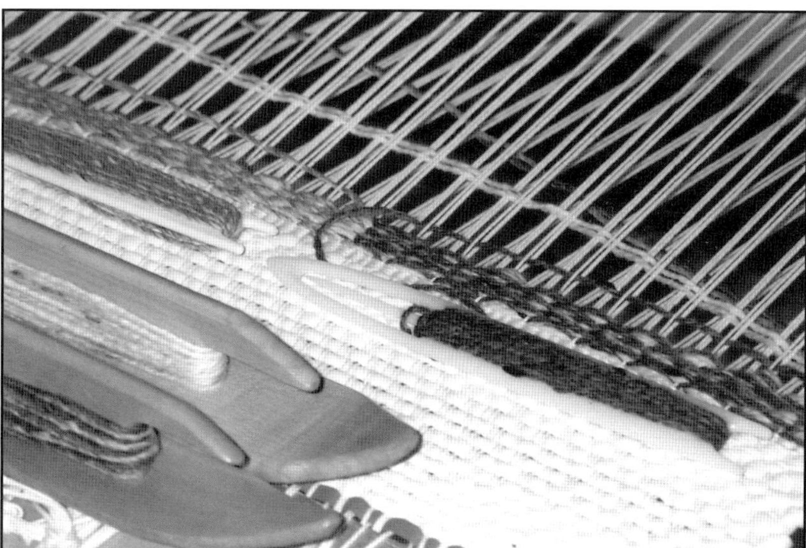

In this photo of a rug on the loom, the pattern weft (on netting shuttles) has been woven; the upper ground is in place behind it; and the lower ground is in back. The weaver is ready to beat all three wefts into place.

Summer Blossoms 36″ x 14″ JH

Winter Roses/Holidays 40″ x 16″ JH

October Leaves 40″ x 14″ JH

Spring Flowers/Pastel Skies **36″ x 16″**

Four seasonal runners follow the wheel of the year. One side is designed with fabric strips or yarns while the other side has a seasonal motif. Summer Blossoms (top of page 86) uses three pattern inlay yarns with a fine ground weft to achieve the intense blue flowers. JH

The Cat's Meow *(below)* **48″ x 21″**

This drawing of a cat had been in my files for many years. Lopi yarns and polar fleece came together when it came time to get this pussy cat off my drawing table and onto the floor! JH

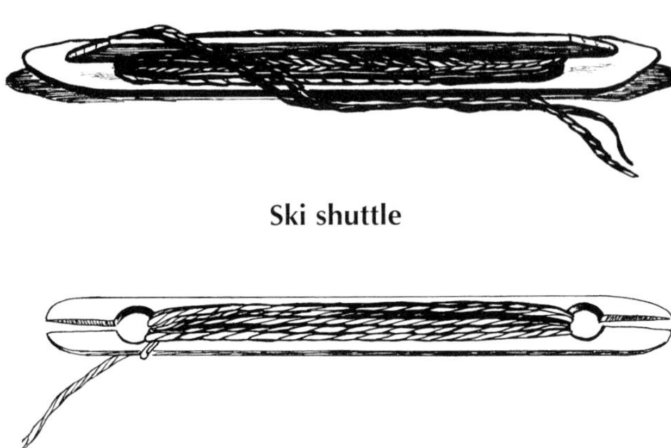

Ski shuttle

Stick shuttle

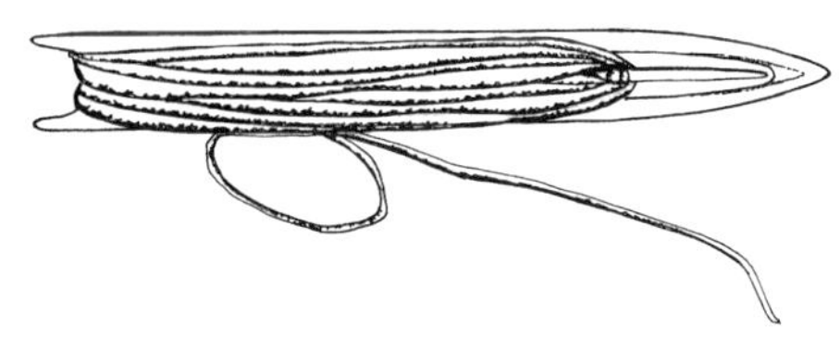

Netting shuttle

Ski shuttles work well for ground weft yarns. Long stick shuttles also work. Netting shuttles are ideal for weaving design areas. The yarn stays better organized than it does in butterflies; netting shuttles help you see which tie-down warp to enter under, and they keep multiple inlay yarns in order.

Weave this structure under high tension. High tension will help you pack the weft as you are weaving. At this point, especially, extra weight on the beater will help you create a solid rug.

Use a cartoon as described in chapter 6. If you are weaving with a temple, the temple will help hold the cartoon in place. But do stitch the cartoon down every six inches to keep it lined up with the warp. The cartoon yet to be used lies in a roll over the temple, while the cartoon that has been used and stitched down is wound onto the cloth beam along with the woven fabric.

Weaving curves

As you begin to weave in double warp overlay, the places where design areas curve can be a challenge. Tie-down warps are farther apart in this variation than they are on other Theo Moorman weaving. The edge of the design area may lie between two tie-down warps. The rule of thumb is that if the design edge is flowing to the right, bring the pattern yarn around the tie-down yarn that is farthest right within the design area. If the design is flowing to the left, bring the pattern yarn out under the tie-down warp that is farthest left within the design area.

Weaving a diagonal line

While the general rule is that inlay design yarns should start from the side where you are treadling (on a floor loom), sometimes better effects can be achieved on a diagonal if the inlay design yarns change direction or are traveling in opposite directions.

Using the sixth shaft

Designs are best realized by using shafts 4 and 5 as the principal tie-down shed. Even though shaft 6 is threaded all the way across the warp, it is not used to create a normal tie-down shed. When the sixth shaft is used across a large pattern area, it disrupts the twill pattern created by using shafts 4 and 5 for pattern inlay. Think of shaft 6 as a supplementary warp thread you can pull up when it is needed to soften a jagged edge, to begin or end design areas, or to achieve better control over points and curves.

When using shaft 6, pick it up at the edge of the design, then go back to the normal pattern shed 4 or 5, whichever follows in your sequence, to inlay the remaining row of pattern inlay.

Once you have completed your first double warp overlay project, you will understand the fascination of this technique and be well on your way to the next one.

Double Warp Overlay for Rugs or Table Runners

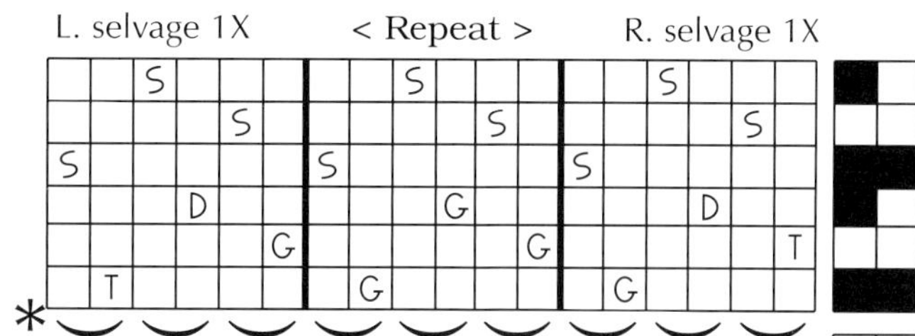

*The half-moon shapes underneath the draft show the sleying order.

T=tripled end of ground warp
D=doubled end of ground warp
G=single end of ground warp
S=single end of pattern warp

X=mock plain weave
P=pattern weft
U=upper ground weft
L=lower ground weft

Sixth shaft when needed

When not weaving the headings, untie the "X" treadles to create spacers.

Rugs and Table Runners

Ends per inch: 8
Reed: 8 dent, sleyed 2, 0
Warp length: Rug length plus 27 inches loom waste, part of which will be used for headings, fringe, or other edging

Rugs

Ground warp: 12/12 cotton seine twine
Tie-down warp: 12/6 cotton seine twine
Ground Weft: upper and lower ground of equal thickness

Table Runners

Ground warp: 5/2 cotton
Tie-down warp: 8/2 cotton
Ground weft: 3/2 cotton, two or three strands each for upper and lower grounds.

Warp Ends Calculation for rugs and table runners

Step 1:
Rug or runner width [*in inches*] x 4 =_____total ends.

Step 2:
Total ends______divided by 3 = ______number of units

Step 3:
Number of units_____x 3 = ______+ 6 =________ total number of ground warp ends

Number of units _____x 3 =______ total number of tie down warp ends

Picks per inch: 12-16 depending on the beat and weft materials used
Take-up and shrinkage will vary according to weft used, but you should allow for least one inch per foot of length.

Double Warp Overlay for A Vest

Mock Plain Weave Vest Back:
Warp: same as front
Ground weft: rose-tone fine wool

Double Warp Overlay Vest Fronts:
Ground warp: 2 ends vanilla Jaggerspun Zephyr silk/wool
Tie-Down warp: 30/3 silk in blue and grey, alternated
Upper ground weft: textured and fine wools
Pattern inlay weft: silk/wools in various colors to achieve the laid in design elements
Lower ground weft: rayon silk ribbon, variegated silk yarns

Joyce was so intrigued by the double warp overlay technique that she wanted to explore its use in clothing. This vest uses the same draft as the previous page. However, she substituted finer warp yarns in place of the heavy cottons.

The back section was woven first with mock plain weave as a square of fabric. The two front sections were woven to shape with a cartoon in the double warp overlay technique to form the reversible vest fronts. Narrow tapes were woven on a belt loom to cover the seams and bind the raw edges. Embellishment with beads and ribbon weft was added. JH

Detail, outside

Detail, inside

Finishing and blocking a rug or table runner

To finish your double warp overlay weaving, make braided or twisted fringed or create a Damascus edge. The Damascus edge illustrated here creates a very clean, formal look.

Damascus edge

Weave a one-half-inch header with the same material used for ground weft or something similar in size. Leave two to three inches of warp ends for pulling in.

Pull the warp ends of the rug up the channels of the rug weft with a fine crochet hook or large tapestry needle.

Vary the distance you pull in the warp yarns so as not to create a ridge where all the warp ends stop at once.

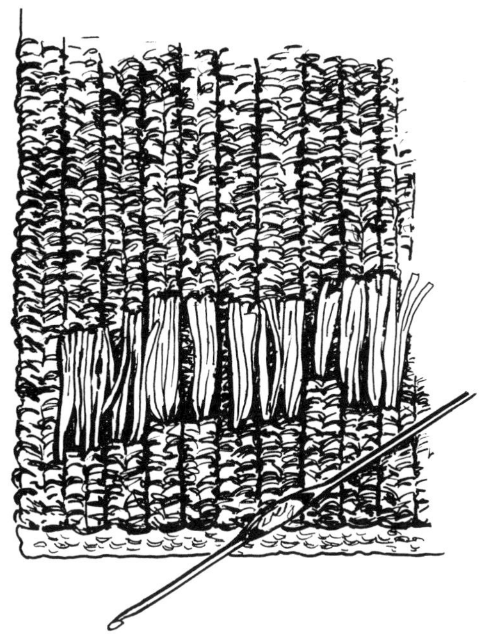

Damascus edge

Another finish

Using the tie-down yarn for weft, weave two inches of mock plain weave on each end of the runner or rug. When the rug or runner is removed from the loom, serge the edge. Then make a triple hem that hides the serged edge; top stitch this hem on the machine. This hem adds to the length of the rug. The hem, because it is triple-folded, will be the same thickness as the rug or runner.

Blocking

It is not necessary to block a runner; steam pressing will be sufficient. However, blocking and steaming will greatly improve a rug by straightening and smoothing it. Although the effects will be most dramatic on weaving made entirely of wool, the blocking process is still an important finishing step for any fiber.

Grid a piece of plywood in square-inch segments using a permanent black marker. It will look like a quilt maker's gridded self-healing mat.

Cover the wood with 4 mm clear plastic.

Using a utility stapler and staples, staple the rug to the board according to the straight lines on the grid. Stretch tight areas and allow loose areas to bulge.

Staple the rug to a gridded sheet of plywood covered with plastic for blocking.

Wet a terry cloth towel until soaked.

Place the towel over the weaving. (Be sure the dye in the yarns will not bleed or run before you begin this steaming process.)

Steam the rug thoroughly using a very hot, dry iron. Re-soak the towel as needed.

Allow the rug to dry thoroughly on the board.

Remove the rug; turn it over; re-staple and steam the other side; allow to dry.

Mock ikat dye-painting for fabric for double warp overlay projects

I saw a rag rug woven with mock ikat painted fabric at the Minneapolis Convergence in 1994 and was taken with it. The weaver was Fritzi Galley. She generously shared her directions. What follows is my adaptation of her steps.

Mock ikat dye-painting is putting your own design onto fabric before cutting it into strips for weft. Fabrics made with this technique can be used for traditional rag rugs and table linens, handwoven clothing, and for double warp overlay projects. Once woven in as ground weft, the design has a watery, impressionist appearance. These directions are for Double Warp Overlay Projects.

Supplies

Procion MX Fiber Reactive Dye powder
Surgical mask or respirator mask
Plastic gloves
Apron
Sodium bicarbonate
Ground cloth
Newsprint paper *(not newspaper)*
Plastic sheeting
Paint brushes or foam brushes
Plastic or glass wide mouth containers
Orvus paste
Guar gum
Quilting ruler
Self-healing rotary mat
Rotary cutter
Quilt thread
Curved needle
100 % cotton fabric
Stick shuttles or ski shuttles
Warp for project
Ground weft and pattern inlay weft

Preparation

1. Wind the warp and prepare the loom.

   Follow the Double Warp Overlay draft in this chapter and warp the loom for your project.

2. Calculate width and amount of fabric.

   These numbers determine how much cloth to dye for weft and how to calculate the dyeing so that the design will reappear when woven.

   Use 100% cotton fabric. I like old cotton sheets purchased from thrift stores because they are wide and dye penetrates them easily. If purchasing new fabric, get 60-inch muslin. Wash new fabric to remove any sizing.

Strip width

Strips will be cut ¼ inch wide.

Fabric width and p.p.i.

Calculate your exact weft width based on your own materials. Cut fabric strips from the un-dyed cloth you are going to use in your project. Weave two inches with this un-dyed fabric weft as upper or lower ground. Use yarn or fabric strips for the other ground. You can leave out pattern inlay for now. Color the selvage edges of the weft with a permanent marker. Unweave the first inch. While unweaving the second inch, count how many picks per inch. This number determines your p.p.i. and will help you determine how much fabric you need. Once the fabric is completely unwoven, measure the average distance between the un-dyed fabric weft strip colored markings. This measurement determines how wide to fold the cloth.

For Springtime/Baby Blocks on page 94, I added two inches to the warp width to make a 38-inch fabric width.

Amount of fabric

I fold the fabric in three layers. If you have more layers, the dye does not penetrate all the layers evenly.

Take the p.p.i times the length of the weaving in inches and divide by 3, so p.p.i. x length/3=length of fabric in inches

For example, for the Springtime/Baby Blocks rug 36″ x 60, ″ the equation was:

8 p.p.i. x 60″ length=480 inches

480/3=160 inches

The final dimensions for the fabric needed for Springtime/Babyblocks rug were 160 inches long x 114 inches wide.

Dye process

1. Preparing the fabric

   Fold the washed fabric into three layers the

width of the finished piece plus two inches. For the rug, I folded the fabric 38 inches wide.

Add as many pieces of folded fabric as needed to reach the correct length.

Iron the fabric to make it perfectly flat and then iron in the creases in the folds.

Using quilting thread and a curved needle, make long running stitches from folded edge to folded edge. Stitch across the fabric every 12 inches. The stitching holds the cloth together through the dyeing and washing.

2. Design

   Plan the design for the fabric. See chapter 4 for design exercises.

   If you are going to put a highly detailed design on the fabric, you may want to use a different color of quilting thread and baste the outline of the design shapes onto the cloth. If you are going to apply a looser type of design, say a field of tulips, then this basting outline won't be necessary.

3. Preparation for dyeing

   Soak the stitched cloth in warm water that has ½ cup of sodium bicarbonate for every gallon of water used. Sodium bicarbonate is basically pure baking soda. I purchase it at feed stores in 25-pound sacks for a fraction of the cost of Pro Activator. Soak the cloth for a minimum of one hour. It doesn't matter how long the cloth stays in. This treatment makes the dye bond to the cloth when it is painted. Spin the cloth out in the spin cycle of the washing machine. Do not rinse. Cloth can then be line-dried or painted on while damp.

4. Prepare dyes

   I use Procion MX fiber reactive dyes in powder form from Pro Chemical and Dye. These dyes come in a wide variety of colors and work well with the cold batching method of curing the fabric.

   When mixing the dye powder, wear a mask, rubber gloves and an apron. Use warm water. For one cup water use ½ teaspoon dye for light shades, one teaspoon dye for medium shades and 2 teaspoons dye for intense shades.

   The dye will have the most potency if used within a month. If you want a thicker paint, add guar gum in small amounts until desired thickness. Guar gum is available in health food stores or the natural food section at the grocery store.

5. Prepare the work surface

   Spread plastic sheeting on the work surface. Lay down a ground cloth. A polyester sheet works well. Lay down newsprint a little wider than the cloth you are painting. Lay out the prepared cloth to be dye painted. If it has wrinkled while drying, iron it flat.

6. Paint and cure

   Use foam or cheap paint brushes to push the dye paint into the cloth as you paint.

   When you have finished painting, put a sheet of newsprint on top of the cloth. Press down over the entire surface to push the dye into all three layers. Roll up the ground cloth, paper, fabric and upper paper like a jelly roll. Place the roll in a plastic bag, seal, and let set at room temperature for at least twelve hours. This process is called cold batching. Fabric could also be steam cured. For steaming instructions see *Synthetic Dyes for Natural Fabrics.*

7. Wash and prepare

   Unroll the fabric. Carefully remove upper paper. Rinse one: take the fabric and wash in cold water. Rinse two: wash in warm water with a small bit of orvus paste. Orvus paste is a gentle soap available at feed stores. Rinse three: wash in warm water. Some colors will wash out a lot. Don't be alarmed. Running is in the nature of fiber reactive dye and cold batching. Put the fabric in the washing machine and spin out in spin cycle. Line dry. Iron the painted fabric, pressing firmly to crease the folded edges. This makes it easy to cut the strips. The folds are the guidelines for placing the fabric strips in the warp. They become the selvages of the rug.

8. Cut and weave fabric strips

Cut the cloth into strips using a rotary cutter, self-healing mat, and a clear plastic quilting ruler. Cut four to six inches at one time. After the first time, you will determine how much will fit onto one shuttle. Keep the strips in order as you glue them with a ⅜-inch overlap. My favorite glue stick is the UHU brand. Wind fabric on a stick or boat shuttle. Weave the strips of fabric as upper ground or lower ground.

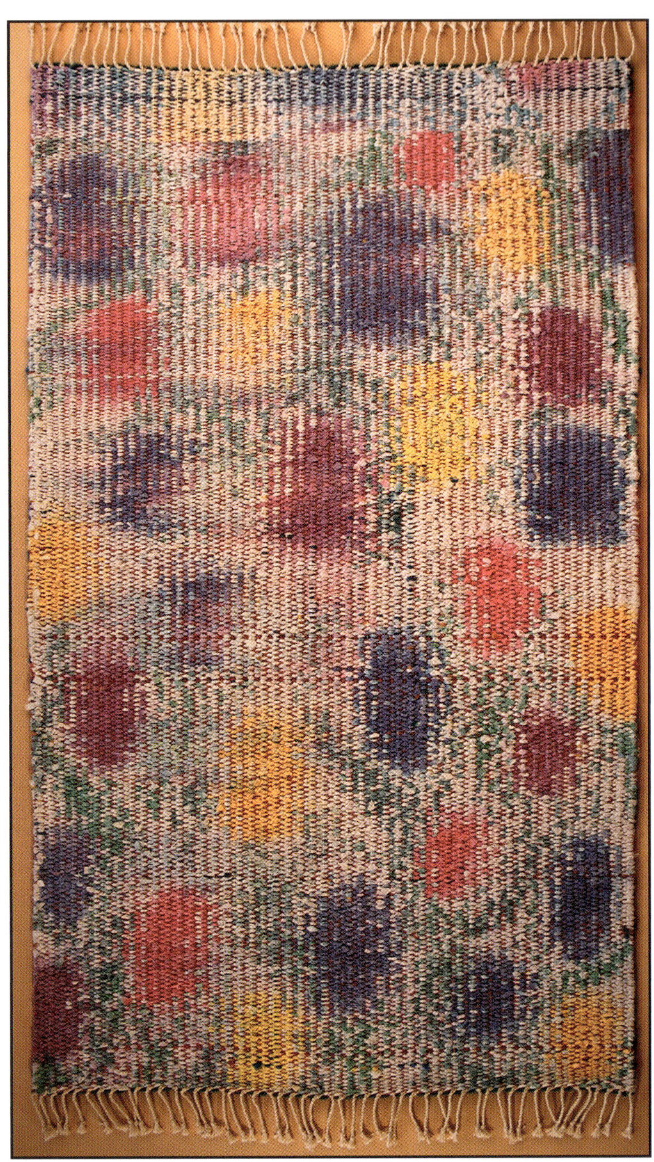

Springtime/Baby Blocks on the Double 3′ x 5′

The wool side of this rug is based on a log cabin quilt pattern. The Halcyon Deco wool yarn is hand-dyed. The reverse side is mock ikat dye-painted cotton fabric. NS

BLUE INTERSECTIONS 3′ x 5′
Both the upper and lower ground weft is mock ikat dye-painted cotton fabric. The geometric pattern inlay design is inlaid with hand-dyed rayon yarn. NS

Chapter 11

Gateways: Exploring the Theo Moorman Technique

Weavers who try the Theo Moorman technique are usually looking for something:

A weave structure that goes beyond pattern and color;
A way to express their ideas and emotions;
A technique that combines their passions for spinning, beads, surface design, or baskets, with loom-woven cloth.

Mary Barker of Brighton, England, had a long friendship with Theo Moorman. Mary wrote to us when we were writing our original book.

> *I actually attended the workshop in her home that she always referred to as the "self-propelling house party." In those days, artist craftsman weavers...were all experimenting with wall hangings using different techniques...She spoke of the technique that bears her name as a "gateway through which weavers could pass to other fields."*

For Mary Barker, for Joyce, for me, and for many other weavers, the Theo Moorman technique has been a gateway for weaving exploration. I love exploring the use of unusual inlay materials and dye techniques and creating sculptural forms. Joyce has developed ways to paint with fabric strips, and to weave double-sided table runners and reversible clothing. What can this weave structure do for your weaving? The versatility of this weave is limited only by the imagination of the weavers who use it. This chapter is an invitation to explore.

Embellishment

Some weavers have gone the direction of augmenting the weave with stitched embellishment. The ground fabric serves well as a foundation for hand and machine embroidery, appliqué, hardanger, or stitched-on braid or trim. Great inspiration for stitched embellishment can be found in the garments created for the annual American Quilters Society fashion show in Paducah, Kentucky, and the Houston International Quilt Festival's Bernina Fashion Show. The magazines Ornament and Belle Armoire are also excellent resources for embellishment ideas and sources. See Resources.

Applied embellishment

Although buttons and beads can be applied after the cloth comes off the loom, these ornaments can be inlaid as pattern weft while weaving. String the buttons or beads on pattern weft yarn or supplemental thread. This thread can be wound onto a netting shuttle and inlaid in selected areas. By starting with pre-strung beads, areas can be inlaid as solid beaded motifs. Pull the beads or buttons out from under the tie-down warps so they stay on the surface of the weaving. The placement of specialty beads—glass, wood, plastic, or traditional clay—may need to be planned so they are used toward the end of the warp where they won't have to wrap around the cloth beam. If bulky beads must be used early in the weaving, pad the cloth beam with bubble wrap or batting as the beads wrap around it.

Unusual pattern wefts

Many weavers recount their great excitement as they tried everything they could think of for pattern weft on their first Theo Moorman sampler. The possibilities are almost unlimited. Anything that will fit under the tie-down weft will work: Lycra, feathers, Ultrasuede, trims, ribbons, Polar Fleece, velvet, raffia, zippers, horsehair and fur. Possibilities are not limited to crushable materials: copper foil, wire, sticks, pine needles, leaves, grasses, seed pods, rocks, coins, buttons, sequins, old jewelry, silverware, paper, dry pasta, tea bags, herbs, flowers.

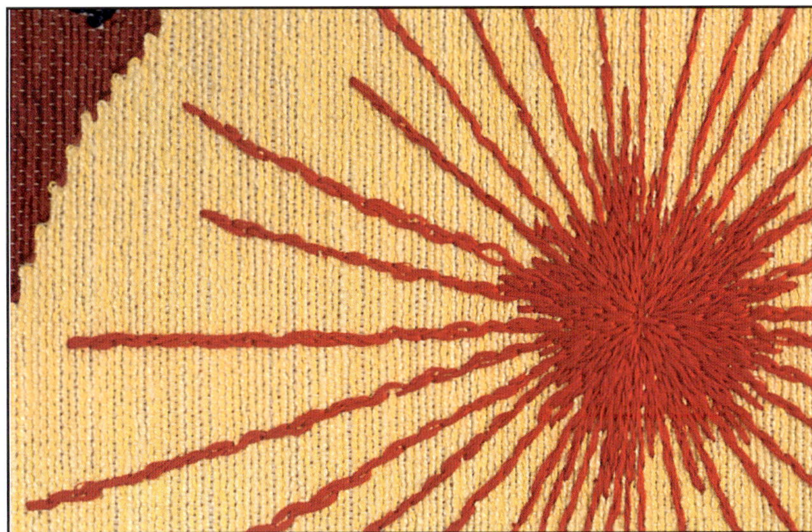

Detail of 23rd Psalm showing hand stitchery added to weaving while it was on the loom. JH

Detail of Website (p. 61) showing stitchery. JH

Detail, wall hanging "Lyngblomsten," Lyngblomsten Home, St. Paul, MN
Stitchery effects can also be created on the loom by carrying the pattern weft from tie-down to tie-down suggesting embroidery on the surface of a piece. JH

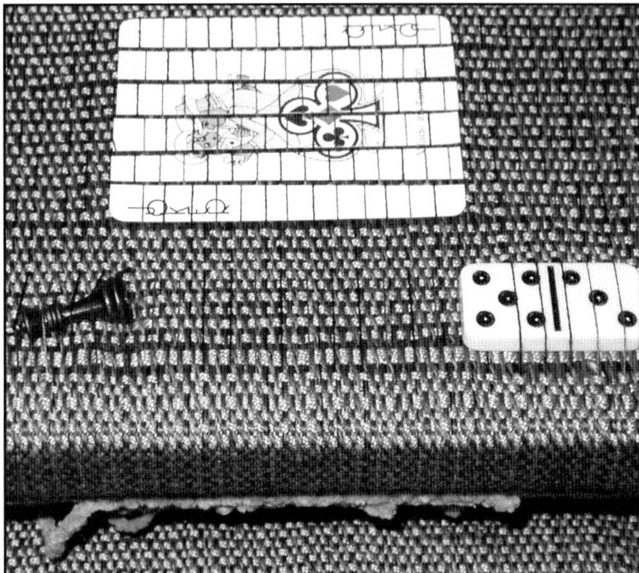

JOKER'S WILD 10½″ x 10″
This sample was woven by a student in a workshop in Columbus, OH.

SCOOBY DOO 10½″ x 8″
This sample was done by a student in a workshop at Fiber Arts Studio in La Habra, CA.

To insert bulky non-crushable items, wrap them with either wire or yarn leaving tails, then inlay the tails. Certain items can have holes drilled into them for threading. Others can be inlaid into a tie-down shed by keeping the tie-down shaft raised, inlaying the object, and then weaving a number of ground picks underneath the object to build up a solid ground. For example, if you are inlaying a piece of bark while shaft 3 is raised, keep 3 raised while throwing ground weft in shed 1-3, keep shaft 3 raised while throwing the ground in shed 2-4; keep shaft 3 raised while weaving as much ground as needed underneath the object. When shaft 3 is finally lowered, the tie-down warps of shaft 3 will have a longer float, but if the object is at least three inches long, it will stay in place in the weaving.

Some weavers have gone the direction of using recycled materials such as plastic bags, plastic wrap, Mylar, foil, candy wrappers, bubble wrap, food containers, balloons, or computer parts. Many large corporations such as Boeing have surplus stores where all sorts of excellent junk can be purchased for recycling into art projects.

If you are working with three-dimensional pattern wefts that can't be wound onto the cloth beam, the length of your piece will be limited to the distance from the reed to the cloth beam. The piece will have to be cut off before it rolls around the cloth beam. If you are often working this way, you can modify your loom by adding an auxiliary rod twelve inches or so below the breast beam that will extend the distance the woven cloth travels before winding onto the cloth beam.

Sculptural forms

Cloth woven in the Moorman technique can be formed off the loom into baskets or other types of sculpture or installation work. Fabric can be formed over an armature. Wire inlaid edge to edge as pattern weft will allow the fabric to be molded like clay. The gauge of the wire determines how stiff the form will be. Certain kinds of wire can also be used as warp. For insight on weaving with wire, see the book *Textile Techniques in Metal for Jewelers, Textile Artists & Sculptors* by Arline Fisch.

A spinners' weave

Spinners eventually come to the point where they have too much yarn to knit. The Moorman technique is an excellent way to show off the luscious fibers or the novelty effects of handspun in handwovens. Inlaying the handspun as pattern weft keeps it on the surface of the fabric where it is seen. Handspun that is scratchy can be inlaid on clothing and won't be felt on the skin because it is on the surface. Bulky handspun can be inlaid in clothing while a supple "hand" is maintained in the ground cloth. Unspun roving or locks of fleece or hair can add texture to a wall hanging or pillow. Handspun singles are excellent upper and lower ground in the double warp overlay technique.

Surface design

The plain background of the Moorman weave is an ideal area for surface design techniques. Stamping, stenciling, screen-printing, airbrushing, foiling, fabric painting, and phototransfer are ways to manipulate the woven cloth. Surface embellishment can add richness and depth to the cloth. When you are designing the woven cloth, take into consideration what surface design techniques you want to use. Then weave extra for sampling. The books, *Color and Design on Fabric* and *Color on Paper and Fabric* are an excellent introduction for a variety of basic surface design techniques.

INLAYING TROLLING LINE

Julie Erick combined fishing trolling line and beads as pattern inlay to experiment with making fabric that can be formed into a basket.

Although the texture of the woven cloth may seem to be more suited to stitchery than paint, warp painting can also be used with the Moorman technique. If you are weaving a dense cloth, it is better to paint directly on the warp after it has been threaded. Weft yarns (ground and pattern) can also be warp-painted to create a mock-ikat effect or illusion of depth. *Surface Design for Fabric* by Richard Proctor and Jennifer F. Lew offers helpful ideas for painting and dyeing. With the Moorman technique, a weaver could use ikat for the ground and tie-down warps, as well as the ground and pattern weft to create truly opulent cloth.

text continues on page 102

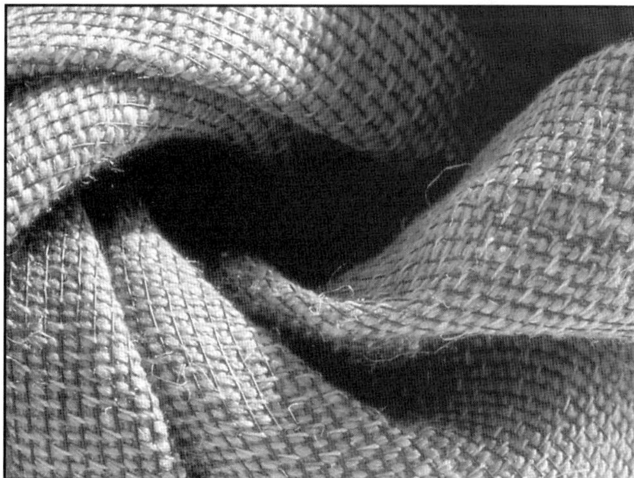

AU SET'S SACKS 17″ X 28″ EACH SACK

The sacks are woven of linen for ground with pattern inlay of annealing wire running from selvage to selvage. Off the loom, the fabric was sewn into bag forms and shaped like clay. NS

Abundance, maturity, Exposure, Urgency

This installation depicts autumn in the Midwest. The season starts with great abundance and ends with bareness. Abundance: Wheat from my father's field. Maturity: Sticks pruned from an apple tree to promote new growth next season. Exposure: Grass withering back into the soil. Urgency: Leaves. No leaves are left on the trees by November when the harvest should be stored in the granary. NS

Lavender Vest with Handspun

Beautiful handspun yarns given to me presented a challenge for clothing. A soft printed silk fabric came to mind for a lining and the design began to take shape. The areas using all of the yarns took various shapes, not trying to complete a circle. Handspun yarn courtesy of Kara Johndro and Norma Ames, spinners. JH

Llama Mama 14″ x 16″

Both handspun and un-spun roving were inlaid in this piece by Barbara Viehman, an avid spinner and weaver.

Adding other structures to the Moorman weave

Another area of exploration is combining Moorman tie-downs with other weave structures. Such variations require a multishaft loom. Weavers have successfully used undulating twill as a background for Moorman designs. Louise Bradley describes the use of an eight-shaft, two-block jeans twill weave with tie-downs for a Moorman design in Handwoven May/June 1994.

Deborah Brandon was a student in one of my workshops. She had just ordered an eight-shaft loom and as soon as it arrived started experimenting with combining Moorman with other structures. She wanted to see if using a twill background and inlaying in a twill would produce a fabric with more drape. She also was interested in trying a plain weave background and a patterned inlay. Further information about her variations is on the CD-ROM.

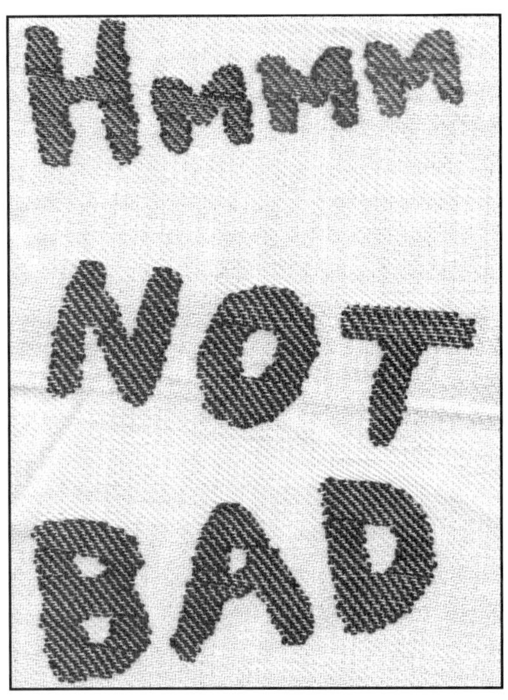

HMMM NOT BAD by Deborah Brandon 10″ x 13″
The ground is 10/2 unmercerized cotton, the tie-down is 20/2 perle cotton, and the inlay a bit finer than 6/2 cotton. The ground and tie-down are threaded for a 2/2 twill. The ground is woven as a 3/3 twill (2 ground plus 1 tie-down) and the inlay is woven as a 2/2 twill.

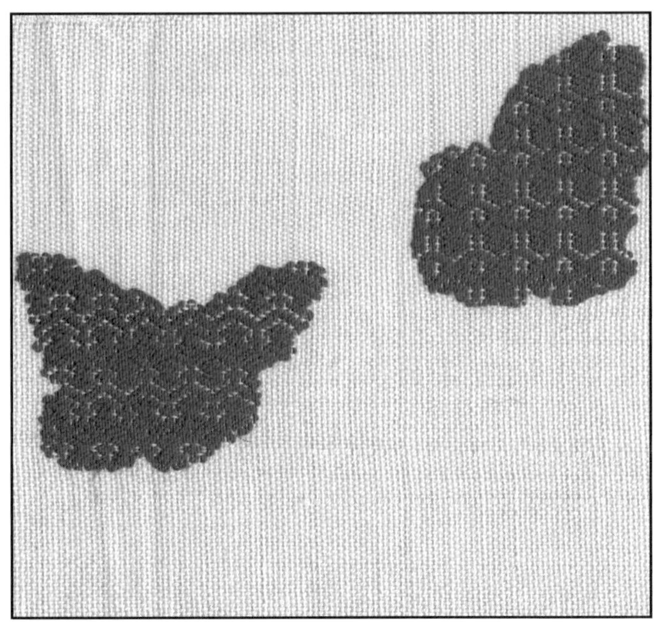

ROSEPATH BUTTERFLIES by Deborah Brandon 9″ x 8″
The ground is threaded for plain weave and the tie-down is threaded for rosepath. The tie-up is plain weave for both ground and tie-down. Different treadling sequences were used for each of the butterflies.

Transparencies

Perhaps the technique most closely related to the Moorman technique is handwoven transparency. Yarn is inlaid on sheer, but stable ground to create areas of opaque and transparent motifs. Combining the Theo Moorman technique with a transparent ground is a wonderful marriage of the two techniques. An excellent book, *Sheer Delight* by Doramay Keasbey, is the resource I recommend. It gives information on design, materials, sett, and finishing of transparencies.

Innovation

Peter Horsfall, of Forest Row, England, was first trained as a violin maker. He then went on to teach woodwork to adults at Emerson College for twenty years. In 1990, Peter reports he was "pushed" into tapestry weaving by his wife, Rachel. Since discovering the Moorman technique he has been innovating in both the structure and in his designs. He works with eight-shaft double-weave with inlay (10 shafts total.) In 1994 he was one of the recipients of the Theo Moorman Charitable trust grant. (See the book, *A Legacy in Weaving: A celebration of the first*

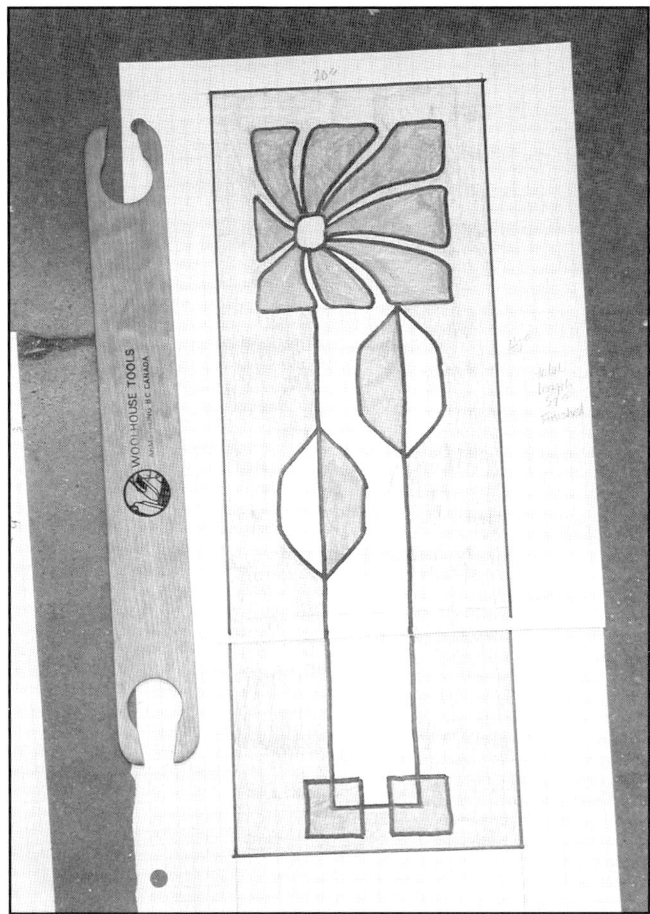

WALL HANGING DESIGN.
A student in a workshop in Vista, CA was interested in transparencies and created this design for a Moorman transparency.

decade of grant-giving by The Theo Moorman Charitable Trust for Weavers.) In his artistic statement, Peter writes:

> *In my weaving the interesting things for me are: the structure of the textile, the particular interlacement and design in this respect of each individual piece; the construction and texture of the fibres and yarns used; the attempt to achieve complete unity of the free-flowing forms of the surface inlay with the more geometric underlying ground weave...I also try to work between the two and three dimensional aspects of artistic expression and this is expressed in the relationship of the fabric to the carved wooden elements.*
>
> *I believe strongly in the necessity of reaching a final essential simplicity by working through phases of complexity. The essence can then bear within it an underlying substance and richness. Without that process of going through complexity and discovery, simplicity for its own sake can be shallow and empty. I want my work to have liveliness, harmony and an underlying rhythmical strength.*

Peter's skillful combination of wood and weaving points to yet another way to integrate other mediums with the Moorman weave.

Conclusion

The Theo Moorman weave served as a gateway to weavers in the twentieth century. The twenty-first century holds techniques and materials yet to be revived and invented. Many weavers have a potluck of weaving skills on their table. Some are just discovering the world of interlaced fibers. This technique is for all of us. It meets us where we are and grows as our design skills, technical skills, imagination, and curiosity move us forward. It could be that in the twenty-first century the memory of the Theo Moorman the weaver will be forgotten. But the spirit of exploration inherent in the nature of this weave will continue to bear the mark of the woman who developed it. The experiments and innovations described in this book are only the beginning of the possibilities that exist within this weave. With work and attention, you can create your own theme and variation and be well on your way to creating weaving that sings.

The Work of Peter Horsfall

Thoughts I 1993. 22″ x 82″ *(left)*
The yarns are cotton and silk; the wood is colored sycamore. In many ancient cultures birds are an outer expression in nature of the human being's inner life in thought.

Klee Weaving 1998. 46″ x 64″ *(lower left)*
The yarns are cotton, linen, and silk; the wood is wire-brushed English oak. Double-weave interchanges on both front and under sides. The idea for this piece came from paintings and sketches of Paul Klee, the Bauhaus artist who was also influential in textile design.

Antipodean Francis 1995. 39″ x 58″
(above; detail bottom of next page)
Yarns are cotton, wool, silk and linen; the wood is colored sycamore. Australian rocks and eucalyptus, aboriginal rock paintings, St. Francis of Assisi with his angel are all part of the inspiration.

Head Bird 1995. 33″ x 23″ *(above and right)*
The yarns used are cotton and wool. The technique is double weave with inlay. The wood elements are English oak, which is shaped, then surface-burnt with a blow-torch, and wire-brushed. Finally the wood is dyed and colored. The shapes of the figures came from the temperaments: melancholic, phlegmatic, sanguine and choleric.

Suitable Warp and Weft Materials

Wall Hangings	Clothing	Rugs	Home Furnishings
Harrisville: 2-ply Highland wool 2-ply Shetland wool 10/2 mercerized cotton 5/2 mercerized cotton 3/2 mercerized cotton Cottolin Silk Rayon DMC perle cotton 8/1 linen 10/2 linen Lyocell	10/2 cotton 5/2 cotton3/2 cotton 5/2 DMC perle cotton Silk: Tussah Cord Bourette Noil Jaggerspun: Zephyr 50/50 silk/wool Heather 100% wool Merino Rayon 8/1 linen 16/2 linen Lyocell	**Double warp overlay:** 8/5 linen 12/12 cotton seine twine 4-ply worsted wool **4-shaft rugs:** 3/2 cotton Carpet warp, cotton 12/6 seine twine	**Double warp overlay runners:** 3/2 cotton 5/2 mercerized or unmercerized **Pillows:** 3/2 cotton 5/2 cotton Lyocell
Tie-down Warp			
20/2 cotton 10/2 cotton Polyester sewing thread Metallic gimp Fine wool Monofilament 30/2, 60/2 Bombyx silk 2-ply reeled Bombyx 60/4 silk-cotton 60/4 silk-ramie	20/2 cotton 8/2 DMC perle cotton 30/3 Guterrman silk thread 45/3 silk	**Double warp overlay:** 8/2 linen 12/6 cotton seine twine 2-ply worsted wool **4-shaft rugs:** 20/2 cotton 10/2 cotton	**Double warp overlay runners:** 8/2 DMC cotton **Pillows:** 20/2 cotton
Ground Weft			
Yarns the same as or similar weight to ground warp to balance weave. 1/2″ strips of fabric	Yarns the same as or similar weight to ground warp to balance weave. Silk ribbon Cotton boucle, flake, slub Wool/rayon crepe Embroidery floss Silks Rayon chenilles Cotton chenilles	**Double warp overlay:** 3/8″ bias-cut Polar Fleece Lopi wool Brown Sheep: Lamb's Pride Bulky Harrisville Highland Wool 1/4″ to 1/2″ bias-cut fabric strips Cotton chenilles Klippan Matt Garn 2- to 3-ply wool Handspun **4-shaft rugs:** 2-,3-, or 4-ply wool 1/2″ fabric strips Chenilles 5/2 or 3/2 cotton in multiples	Yarns the same as or similar weight to ground warp to balance weave. **Double warp overlay runners:** 3/2 cotton in multiples 5/2 cotton in multiples

Suitable Warp and Weft Materials

Pattern Inlay Weft
The variety is so great for pattern inlay weft that only general materials are listed here. Alpaca, Angora, Camel, Cashmere, Cotton, Cottolin, Linen, Llama, Qivuit, Ramie, Rayon, Silk, Synthetics, Tencel (lyocell), Wool Objects from nature, synthetic objects

Setts for Multi-layered Inlay

Choosing a sett depends on how much detail you have in your design; the more intersections you have, the more detail you can have.

Ends Per Inch	Ground Warp	Tie-down Warp	Reed	Increment
18	12	6	12 2 ground alternating with 1 tie-down	5/16"
24	16	8	12 3-1-2 3=2 ground + 1 tie-down 1=1 tie-down 2=2 grounds	4/16"
27	18	9	14 2 warps in every dent: ground + tie-down ground + tie-down 2 ground repeat this sequence	3/8"
36	24	12	12 3, 1, 2 3=2 ground + 1 tie-down 1=1 tie-down 2=2 ground	3/8"

Glossary

Airbrush: a tool used to apply dyes or paints where soft or graded effects are desired. Requires air supply, air hose and airbrush itself.

Appliqué: the process of sewing or attaching elements, usually pieces of fabric, to a base or ground.

Ark curtain: hangs in front of the enclosure in a synagogue or temple for the scrolls of the torah.

Batik: a surface design technique involving melted wax resists and applying dye in the non-resist areas.

Beater: on a loom, the framework that supports the reed. The beater swings freely between the shafts and the breast beam to pack the weft yarn into position.

Bias: fold the fabric until the lengthwise grain is parallel to the crosswise grain. The fold line is the true bias.

Boat shuttle: yarn is wrapped on a bobbin and then feeds out automatically as the shuttle is thrown through the shed.

Breast beam: also called front beam. A flat beam used to elevate and level the warp for weaving. It is higher and outside of the cloth beam.

Butterfly: miniature skein of weft yarn wound around the fingers.

Cartoon: a drawing traced from a full-scale paper design onto featherweight non-fusible interfacing. It is used as a guide for pattern inlay wefts. It is fastened to the upper surface of the weaving to act as a "road map."

Castle: uppermost part of the loom framework, which supports the harnesses.

Chaining the warp: looping the warp on itself to prevent tangling when the warp is being transferred from the warping frame to the loom.

Challah cover: A cloth cover for the traditional braided bread used for the Jewish Sabbath.

Chasuble: the principal outer vestment used by the presiding minister celebrating the Eucharist in a Christian church.

Chuppah: wedding canopy used in Jewish weddings.

Cloth beam: across the front of the loom, halfway up, a large rotating beam where the cloth as fabric is rolled up as it is woven.

Colcha: coverlet or quilt; the stitch is found on embroidered bedspreads in the American southwest.

Commissions: order something special, place an order for something that must be specially made or created.

Cope: a cape worn in procession at non-Eucharistic ceremonies in place of the chasuable.

Cross: the point where the warp yarns are alternated around pegs on a warping frame or reel during the warping operation. The cross maintains the correct sequence of yarns. Also called the **lease cross, thread-by-thread cross or weavers cross**. A second cross can be made in the other end of the warp. This is called the **raddle cross**.

Crossover: Two pattern weft shuttles in the same shed cross over each other.

Dalmatic: garment worn by the deacon in a Christian church.

Damascus edge: a foundation for weaving the warp ends back into the cloth.

Dent: one space in a reed.

Double weave: a weave that simultaneously produces two distinct layers of cloth, interpenetrating at some point.

Double warp overlay: double weave with an additional pattern layer on top of the upper layer.

Draft: graphic representation of threading, treadling, tie-up, or structure of a weave. It can be all of the above.

Drape: the manner in which cloth hangs or is cut to hang, as in a garment.

Dye-painting: Painting dye directly on the fabric.

Embellishment: the addition of braids, beading, embroidery, applique or rows of stitching to enhance a piece of clothing or wall hanging.

End-feed shuttle: When the shuttle is caught, thread stops coming off the bobbin. The stationary bobbin allows the weaver to obtain a clean selvage edge more easily.

Ends: individual warp yarns.

E.P.I.: ends per inch.

Foamcore board: a rigid white foam core panel, available in various thickness, coated on both sides with white or colored paper. It is easily cut and lightweight.

Fell line: the point during the process of weaving where the woven fabric meets the unwoven warp. It changes with each pick placed.

Fibonacci series: a design sequence based on a mathematical progression in which each number is the sum of the preceding numbers.

Float: any portion of a warp or weft yarn that extends without intersection over two or more units of the opposing set of yarns.

Foiling: to decorate with metallic foil.

Friction brake: sometimes used on the warp beam, a round piece of metal held tight by a cable.

Full spectrum lighting: replicates all the wavelengths in the visible spectrum of sunlight in the same proportions as natural light.

Funeral pall: A large piece of fabric used to cover the bare casket when a funeral takes place in a church.

Fusible web: a web-like fabric of glue strewn in a fibrous thin layer that melts and bonds when heated.

Gimp: flat tinsel wound around a soft core.

Ground weft: in the Moorman technique, the yarn that weaves the background.

Guar gum: gum extracted from the seeds of the guar plant, added to processed food as a thickener and stabilizer used in paper manufacturing and to thicken dye.

Hand: the touch or feel of a fabric.

Hardanger embroidery: Scandinavian counted thread embroidery, traditionally done with white thread on white fabric.

Harness: a set of shafts.

Hot or cold shrink: a method of finishing fabric involving wetting and steaming; also known as **London shrink**.

Heddle: a wire, strip of metal, or cord with an eye. One of more warp yarns pass through the eye. The heddles control the separation of the warp threads and create a shed.

Ikat: process of resist dying portions of a warp, weft, or both, before weaving to create a pattern.

Interfacing: a stabilizing layer used to prevent stretching and to add body to garment edges and to detail areas.

Interrupt: large areas of a second color are placed on the background pattern inlay.

Jack loom: a floor loom in which each shaft operates independently.

Kippah: skullcap; a head covering worn by Jews.

Lam: bar connecting shafts to treadles on a floor loom; also **lamm.**

Lease sticks: pair of smooth, flat sticks used to maintain the cross in the warp yarn.

Lining: A layer of fabric cut and sewn separately from the woven fabric. It covers inside construction, makes garments easier to slip on and off and adds more body to the garment.

Liturgical weaving: cloth pieces used on the altar or in the chancel area of a church or worn by clergy for a worship setting.

Lower ground: the bottom layer when weaving the double warp overlay technique. Created by raising sheds 2-3-5-6 or 1-3-4-6.

Lycra: a spandex fiber used in athletic apparel.

Miter: ceremonial hat for a Christian bishop.

Mixed warp: a warp made with a variety of different yarns.

Mock ikat dye-painting: applying dye to fabric to create weft effect ikat coloring similar to weft ikat dyed yarn.

Monofilament: an untwisted and continuous single strand of natural or artificial fiber such as nylon, often used for fishing line.

Multi-layered inlay: a variation of the Theo Moorman technique that uses fabric strips as pattern inlay weft. A second layer of yarn may be inlaid over the top of the fabric strips.

Multishaft weaving: looms having more than four shafts.

Mylar: a trademark for a polyester film made by Dupont which is an excellent barrier to gas and water vapor, as well as being flexible and puncture resistance.

Netting Shuttle: plastic or sometimes wooden shuttle originally used for making and mending fishing nets. It has a curved point at one end and has a thin tongue to wrap yarn around.

Novelty yarn: yarn characterized by irregularities of size, twist, or effect.

Opaque: not transparent; dull or dark.

Opaque effect: the pattern inlay weft is the same size or slightly larger than the ground weft. Designs will appear solid and no ground will show through.

Orvus paste: a soap known as sodium lauryl sulfate. A soft solid when cool. Melts to amber liquid when warm. Used to wash fabric and yarn.

Parament: A generic name for any fabric hangings used on the altar, pulpit, lectern, or credence table of a church.

Pattern inlay weft: in the Moorman technique, the yarn that weaves the design or pattern.

Phototransfer: Any method by which a photographic image is transferred to cloth.

Pick: see shot.

P.P.I.: picks per inch.

Plain beam: a rotating beam on the back of the loom. Unwoven warp winds around it as opposed to **sectional beam**-a beam divided into sections with metal clips or wooden pegs.

Ply yarn: yarn in which two or more strands are twisted together

Polarfleece: the trademark name of fleece produced by Malden Mill Industries. Fleece is a warm fabric with a thick pile.

Raddle: wooden lath with vertical pegs, set on back beam during warping, to spread warp evenly when warping back to front.

Ratchet brake wheel: used on both cloth and warp beams, a brake that rolls freely in one direction but is prevented from turning back by slanting teeth.

Reed: straight row of evenly spaced metal blades set into the beater of the loom. The reed helps to maintain the horizontal position of the warp yarns and beats each new weft yarn into position.

Rotary cutter: a tool used for cutting fabric and paper. A handle is attached to a round metal blade.

Roving: fiber that has been prepared for spinning, but as yet unspun.

Rya: Scandinavian pile weave.

Saturated effect: using very thick pattern inlay yarns, much thicker than the ground weft.

Screen-printing: technique for printing stencil designs. A stencil pattern is applied to and supported by the screen. Paint or ink is forced through the screen onto the surface to be decorated.

Selvage: lengthwise or warpwise edge of a woven fabric; the edge at which the weft yarns bind the warp.

Sett, set: the density of a fabric; the number of warp yarns per inch.

Shaft: an individual frame with heddles on it which moves the warp yarns up and down.

Shed: the angle between the two parts of the warp, through which the weft yarn is passed. A shed is created by raising one or more shafts.

Shot: one passage of the weft yarn through the shed; same as **pick**.

Singles: a yarn composed of only one strand.

Ski shuttle: used for holding heavy yarns.

Sleying: drawing the warp yarns through the reed.

Stencil: a method of transferring an image or design to the surface.

Stick shuttle: a flat piece of wood with a curve or notch on each end, used to carry yarns through the shed.

Stole: A long, narrow garment worn by clergy to denote their status as clergy.

Stretcher: see **temple**.

String cradle: Cords or strings attached to the back beam of the loom to hold the supplemental rod when spreading the warp. These short cradles also hold the back apron rod. Additional long string cradles for lease sticks hang from the castle.

Supplementary rod: a ⅜-inch rod of stainless steel slipped through the uncut ends of a warp and attached to the back apron rod.

Surface design: hand processes used to embellish or alter fabric, paper or other non-textiles.

Tabernacle veil: A curtain to cover the door of the tabernacle where the consecrated bread is kept in a Catholic church.

Take-up: reduction in width or length of fabric while weaving; extra yarn allowance needed to compensate for this reduction.

Tailor: To make clothes to meet a particular need or for a particular person.

Tailored: marked by a neat fit with trim lines and a clean and formal or severe look.

Tallit: a traditional prayer shawl worn at a Jewish synagogue.

Tapestry: weft-faced plain weave fabric in which the weft yarns are discontinuous.

Tapestry comb: wooden or metal tool with teeth, often weighted, for packing down weft.

Tencel: brand name for lyocell. Lyocell is a modern, environmentally responsible version of rayon, made with 99% recycled fiber wood pulp.

Tension: tautness of warp yarns.

Temple: device for maintaining consistent width of fabric on the loom; two flat pieces of wood or metal, either hinged or sliding on each other, with sharp points on the ends. Same as **stretcher**.

Tessellation: repeating geometric patterns that transform as the space between the repeats changes.

Theo Moorman weave: a plain weave derivative named after the weaver Theo Moorman. Having two sets of warp yarns, one smaller than the other which allows pattern yarns to be inlaid on the surface of the fabric.

Thrums: the unweavable portion of the warp yarns required for tying on the loom. Also called **loom waste**.

Tie-down warp: thin warp yarn used in the Theo Moorman technique, usually 20/2 cotton threaded on shafts 3 and 4.

Tie-up: order in which treadles are tied to lams.

Torah cover: the cloth covering of the holy scroll of the Jewish people.

Transparency: delicacy and lightness, contrasting opaque areas of decorative inlay with the sheer fabric of the background.

Transparent effect: the pattern inlay yarn is significantly thinner than the ground weft. When inlaying transparent designs, you will still be able to see the ground through design area.

Treadle: a foot lever that controls the raising of shafts on a floor loom.

Tufting Needle: a three-inch long heavy needle with a curved, wedged, sharp point.

Turn-arounds: when pattern weft yarns go around the finer warp yarns to create design edges.

Ultraseude: trademark of a microfiber fabric made by Toray. A synthetic, non-woven material with a suede surface used for clothes and upholstery.

Upper ground: in double warp overlay, the layer created by raising shafts 2-5 or 1-4.

Variegated yarn: marked with different colors in spots or streaks.

Veil and burse: Veil: covering for the chalice before and after Eucharist. Burse: a stiff, square fabric case used as a holder for the corporal.

Velcro: brand name for hook and loop tape used to stick things together.

Warp: a set of yarns, placed on the loom under tension before weaving begins, parallel to one another and to the selvage or longer dimension of a woven fabric; the lengthwise element in a woven piece.

Warp beam: a large rotating beam halfway up on the back of the loom. The warp is rolled around it before weaving.

Warp-painting: applying dye to yarn either before it is warped or after it is wound and threaded on the loom.

Warping paddle: a piece of wood or plastic shaped like a paddle. Holes and slots allow for winding up to twenty warp yarns in one pass.

Waulking: fulling of the cloth by hand, traditionally accompanied by Gaelic songs.

Weave-under: a small shape is placed in the middle of a field of another color.

Weft: set of yarns or other material at right angles to the selvage; the crosswise element in a woven construction.

Bibliography

Introduction

Harter, Joyce and Nadine Sanders. *Weaving That Sings: Variations on the Theo Moorman Technique.* Northfield, MN: Loomis Studio, 1994
ISBN 0964431505

Moorman, Theo. *Weaving As An Art Form: A Personal Statement.* New York: Van Nostrand Reinhold Co., 1975.
ISBN 0442260024

Chapter 1

Hilary Diaper, editor. *Theo Moorman 1907-1990 Her Life and Work as an Artist Weaver.* Leeds: University Gallery, 1992.

Diaper, Hilary, editor. *A Legacy in Weaving: A celebration of the first decade of grant-giving by The Theo Moorman Charitable Trust for Weavers.* Leeds: The University Gallery Leeds, 2001.
ISBN 187433126X

Chapter 3

Klein, Barry and Laura Militzer Bryant. *Knitting With Novelty Yarn.* Woodinville, WA: Martingale & Co., 2001
ISBN 1564773574

Chapter 4

Edward, Betty. *The New Drawing on the Right Side of the Brain.* New York: Jeremy P. Tarcher/Putnam, 1999.
ISBN 0874774195 hardcover
ISBN 0874774241 paperback

Cameron, Julia. *The Artist's Way: A Spiritual Path to Higher Creativity.* New York: Penguin Putnam, 2002.
ISBN 1585421464

Goldberg, Natalie and Judith Guest. *Writing Down the Bones: Freeing the Writer Within.* Boston: Shambhala, 1986.
ISBN 0877733759

Wong, Wucious. *Principles of Color Design: Designing with Electronic Color.* New York : John Wiley & Songs, Inc., 1997.
ISBN 0471287083

Kurtz, Carol. *Designing for Weaving: A Study Guide for Drafting, Design and Color.* New York: Hastings House, 1981.
ISBN 0803815794
Although it is out of print,this book is still available used online and from libraries.

Chijiiwa, Hideaki. *Color Harmony: A Guide to Creative Color Combinations.* Rockport, MA: Rockport Publishers, 1987
ISBN 0935603069

Holtzschue, Linda. *Understanding Color An Introduction for Designers.* New York: Van Nostrand Reinhold, 1995.
ISBN 0442016832

Eiseman, Leatrice. *Pantone Guide to Communicating with Color.* Sarasota, FL: Grafix Press, Ltc., 2000.
ISBN: 0966638328

Maisel, Eric. *The Creativity Book: A Year's Worth of Inspiration and Guidance.* New York: J.P. Tarcher/Putnam, 2000.
ISBN 1585420298

Maisel, Eric. *Fearless Creating: A Step-By-Step Guide to Starting and Completing Your Work of Art.* New York: Putnam, 1995.
ISBN 0874778050

Sark. *Succulent Wild Woman: Dancing With Your Wonder-Full Self!* New York: Simon & Schuster, 1997.
ISBN 068483376X

Chapter 5

Voiers, Leslie. *Winding Multi-Colored Warps with a Warping Paddle.* Harrisville, NH: Water's Edge Weaving Studio, 1996.

Johnston, Ann. *Color By Design: Paint and Print with Dye.* Lake Oswego, OR: Ann Johnston, 2001.
ISBN 0965677613

Chapter 6

Selfridge, Gail. *Graph It!* Loveland, CO: Interweave Press, 1991.
ISBN 0934026726
Although this book is currently out of print, it is available used online and from libraries.

Sanders, Nadine. *Warping On a Shoestring.* Chehalis, WA: The Singing Weaver, 2002.
ISBN 0972024808

Chapter 7

Harter, Joyce and Lucy Brusic. *Weaving For Worship.* McMinnville, OR: Robin and Russ Handweavers, Inc.,1998.
ISBN 1566590566

Chapter 8

Do-It-Yourself Fabric Décor: Pillows, Window Treatments and Slipcovers for Your Home. Minnetonka, MN: Creative Publishing International, 2000.
ISBN 0865733457

Johnson-Srebro, Nancy. *Rotary Magic: Easy Techniques to Instantly Improve Every Quilt You Make.* Emmaus, PA: Rodale Press, 1998.
ISBN 0875967833

Martin, Judy. *Judy Martin's Ultimate Rotary Cutting Reference.* Grinnell, Iowa: Crosley-Griffith, 1992
ISBN 0929589041

Chapter 9

West, Virginia. *Designer Diagonals: Portfolio of Patterns for Bias Clothing.*
Baltimore: Virginia West, 1988.

Burnham, Dorothy K. *Cut My Cote.* Toronto: Royal Ontario Museum, 1973

Winslow, Heather Lyn. *More On Moorman: Moorman Inlay Adapted to Clothing.* Sugar Grove, IL: Heather Winslow, 1994.
ISBN 096321070X

Ericson, Lois with Anne Charles. *Opening and Closing.* Salem, OR: Eric's Press, 1996
ISBN 0911985093

The following three books on loom-shaped cloth ing and sewing are out of print but may be available from guild or public libraries.

Mayer, Anita Luvera. *Clothing From The Hands That Weave.* Loveland: CO: Interweave Press, 1984
ISBN 0934026149

Beard, Betty J. *Fashions From the Loom: Handwoven Clothing Made Easy.* Loveland, CO: Interweave Press, 1980.
ISBN 0934026033

Alderman, Sharon D and Kathryn Wertenberger. *Handwoven, Tailormade: A Tandem Guide To Fabric Designing, Weaving, Sewing, and Tailoring.* Loveland, CO: Interweave Press, 1982.
ISBN 0934026084

Curtis, Linda Kubik. *Sew Something Special: Sewing With Handwoven Fabrics.* San Jose, CA: Well Dressed Publications, 1996.
ISBN 0965333736

Podolak, Cecelia. *Easy Guide to Sewing Jackets.* Newton, CT: Taunton Press, 1995.
ISBN 1561581100

Chapter 10

Collingwood, Peter. *The Techniques of Rug Weaving.* New York: Watson-Guptill Publications, 1968.

Hand, Barbara, "Rug Weaving: One Weaver's Approach." *Weavers Journal* (Spring 1983): 32-38.

Harter, Joyce B. "Double Warp Overlay for Rugs." *Handwoven* (Nov.-Dec. 1993): 64-66.

Allen, Heather L. *Weaving Contemporary Rag Rugs: New Designs, Traditional Techniques.* Asheville, NC: Lark Books, 1998.
ISNB 1-887374-39-6

Ligon, Linda C. editor with Marilyn Dillard…et al. *A Rug Weaver's Source Book: A Compilation of Rug Weaving.* Loveland, CO: Interweave Press, 1984.
ISBN 0935026165

Johansson, Lillemor, Pia Wedderien, Marie Roland editors. *Swedish Rag Rugs 35 New Designs.* Trellborg: VävMagasinet, 1995.
ISBN 919713161X

Meany, Janet and Paula Pfaff. *Rag Rug Handbook.* Loveland, CO: Interweave Press, 1996.
ISBN 188310 284

Samuel, Cheryl. *Celtic Line Drawing, Workbook One: Plaitwork.* Sangudo, Alberta: Cougar Wright Crossing, Inc., 2000
ISBN 0968678432

Knutson, Linda. *Synthetic Dyes for Natural Fabrics.* Loveland: Co: Interweave Press, 1986.
ISBN 0934026238

Chapter 11

Color and Design on Fabric. Minnetonka, MN: Creative Publishing International, 2000.
ISBN 0865738696 hardcover
ISBN 086573870X softcover

Fisch, Arline. *Textile Techniques in Metal for Jewelers, Textile Artists & Sculptors.* Asheville: Lark/Sterling, 1996.
ISBN 0937274933

Issett, Ruth. *Color on Paper and Fabric: A Wealth of Techniques For Applying Color.* London: B.T. Batsford, Ltd, 1998
ISBN 1893164020

Proctor, Richard and Jennifer F. Lew. *Surface Design for Fabric.* Seattle: University of Washington Press, 1995.
ISBN 029597446X

Eichorn, Rosemary. *The Art of Fabric Collage.* Newtown, CT: Taunton Press, 2000.

Bradley, Louise. "Theo Moorman Inlay Technique." *Handwoven* (May-June 1994): 32-33, 75-76.

Keasbey, Doramay. *Sheer Delight—Handwoven Transparencies.* Petaluma, CA: Stellar Publishing House, Inc., 1990.
ISBN 0962346837

Horsfall, Peter. "Journey Into Weaving." Journal for Weavers, Spinners & Dyers (June 1997): 28.

Diaper, Hilary, editor. *A Legacy in Weaving: A celebration of the first decade of grant-giving by The Theo Moorman Charitable Trust for Weavers.* Leeds: The University Gallery Leeds, 2001.
ISBN 187433126X

Glossary

Encarta World English Dictionary. http://dictionary.msn.com/. 2002.

Magazine Articles

Alderman, Sharon. "Squares on Squares Blouse." *Handwoven* (May-June 1994): 41, 79-81.

Barrett, Clotilde. "Theo Moorman's Inlay Techniques." *Weavers' Journal* (July 1976): 5-7.

Bradley, Louise. "Flame-Bordered Coat in Moorman Technique." *Handwoven* (Nov-Dec. 1992): 49; 86-87.

———. "Tibetan Turquoise Vest." *Handwoven* (May-June 1994): 32-33; 75-76.

Chadwick, Eileen. "A Tribute to Theo Moorman MBE." *The Journal for Weavers, Spinners & Dyers* (July 1990).

Chittenden, Anne. C. "A Journey in Progress." *Shuttle Spindle & Dyepot* (Fall 1986): 50-59.

Collingwood, Peter. "A Conversation with Theo Moorman." *Handwoven* (Jan.-Feb. 1989): 15-20.

———. "Craftnotes, Obituaries: Theo Moorman." *Crafts* (May/June 1990): 13.

"Conversation with Theo Moorman." *Fiberarts* (July-August 1976): 22.

Dunwell, Anna. "Theo Moorman: Experiments in Weaving" (exhibit). *Fiberarts* (Sept.-Oct. 1982): 80.

Edwards, Bertie. "All My Houses in Theo Moorman." *Weaver's* (Volume 24): p.33.

Harter, Joyce. "Vest With a Design Edge." *Weaver's* (Spring 1998): 16-18.

Harter, Joyce and Nadine Sanders. "Celtic Twist Two." *Weaver's* (Volume 42): pp 66-67, 76.

Herring, Connie. "Lilies on an Antique tray." *Prairie Wool Companion* (Nov. 1984): 30-31.

Holroyd, Ruth N. "The Theo Moorman Technique." *Handwoven* (Jan.-Feb. 1989): 61-64.

Horsfall, Peter. "*Structure With Bach on the Loom.*" The Journal for Weavers, Spinners & Dyers (March 1999): 24.

Hoskins, Nancy Arthur. "Moorman Weave Variations." *Shuttle Spindle & Dyepot* (Winter 1981): 6-9.

Liebler, Barbara. "Designing from the Hearth." *Handwoven* (March-April 1988): 64-68.

Marston, Ena. "Theo Moorman: English Tapestry Weaver in San Francisco. *Hand-weaver and Craftsman* (Winter 1969): 12-13; 36.

"Moorman Technique." *Handwoven* (Jan. 1982): 38.

Moorman, Theo. "Poet on the Loom." *Shuttle Spindle & Dyepot* (Fall 1975): 15.

————. "Weaving Small Objects." *The Weavers Journal* (Winter 1976): 19-22.

Norrie, Jane. "Theo Moorman: Jane Norrie Salutes the Woman and her Work." *Crafts* (Sept.-Oct. 1987): 40-41.

Paul, Jan. "Weaving Works for Worship." *Weavers' Journal* (Summer 1981): 40-41.

Reynolds, Judy. "Purple Haze Vest." *Handwoven* (May-June 1994): 42; 81-82.

Searle, Karen. "Moorman Inlay Technique." *Prairie Wool Companion* (Nov. 1981): 30.

Selk, Karen. "Inspiration—Idea—Accomplishment." *Handwoven* (Jan.-Feb. 1991): 81-83.

————. "A Kimono/Pant Ensemble." *Weavers' Journal* (Spring 1984): 72-74.

Swafford, Sandra. "Floral Gift Wrap." *Handwoven* (May-June 1994): 34; 40; 76.

Sylvan, Katherine, "Cocoon in Moorman Weave." *Handwoven* (March-April 1988): 61.

————. "A Tale of a Talis." *Weavers' Journal* (Summer 1981): 42-45.

"Theo Moorman Charitable Trust 1996 Awards. "*The Journal for Weavers, Spinners, Dyers.*" (March 1998): 16.

"Theo Moorman Award Reports." *The Journal for Weavers, Spinners, Dyers.*" (June 2000): 35.

Tremblay, Gail. "The Weavings of Elizabeth Walker: A Personal Exploration of Women's Lives Using the Apron as Metaphor." *Calyx* (Winter 1992-93): 40-44.

Waller, Irene. "Theo Moorman." *Shuttle Spindle & Dyepot* (Fall 1986): 60.

"Where Are They Now?" *Fiberarts* (Jan.-Feb. 1990): 21.

Winslow, Heather. "Moorman Inlay for Clothing." *Weaver's*. (Summer 1989): 22-25.

Resources

I refer to certain tools and materials by brand names, because these are the specific materials and tools that I have found work well with this technique. The brands and company's mentioned have not asked to be included in this book nor have they contributed monetarily to the creation of this book. When I recommend a certain retailer, unless they are an exclusive dealer, it is because I have found that their customer service exceeds their competitors.

Introduction

Lucy Brusic
Editor/designer/writer
2134 Knapp Street
St. Paul, MN 55108
Tel: (651) 646-2970
Email: lucybrusic@aol.com
lucybrusic@visi.com

Joyce Harter
513 Loomis Court
Northfield, MN 55057
Tel: (507) 645-5079
Email: hloomis@rconnect.com

I Weave What I Believe
Owner/Artist/Weaver: Barbara Berg
Address: 407 Leif Erickson Drive
City/State/Zip: Decorah, IA. 52101
Tel: (563) 382-5727
Fax: (563) 387-0770
Liturgical weaving commissions: Paraments, stoles, chasuables, tapestries, funeral palls, burse and veil, fair linens

Straw Into Gold
P.O. Box 268
Chehalis, WA 98532
Web: www.singingweaver.com/strawintogold
Musical ensemble focused on vocal harmony

Chapter 2

The Singing Weaver
P.O. Box 268
Chehalis, WA 98532
Tel: (360) 740-0914
Fax: (360) 740-5517
Web: www.singingweaver.com
Netting Shuttles: Small 5″, Medium 6″, Large 8″
Shoestrings: Polyester, 27″

Chapter 3

Harrisville Designs
Center Village
Post Office Box 806
Telephone: (603) 827-3333
Toll free (800) 338-9415
Fax: (603) 827-3335
Web: http://www.harrisville.com/
Shetland and Highland wool yarns

Webs
P.O. Box 147
Northhampton, MA 01061-0147
Tel: (413) 584-2225
Toll Free: (800) 367-9327
Fax: (413) 584-1603
Web: http://www.yarn.com/
Wool crepe yarn

Yarns and...
201 Park Avenue
Second Floor
Birmingham, MI 48009-3404
Tel: (248) 647-2400
Toll Free: (800) 520-YARN
Web: http://www.yarns-and.com/
Trendsetter novelty knitting yarns plus many other knitting yarns

Chapter 4

Elderhostel
11 Avenue de Lafayette
Boston, MA 02111-1746
Toll Free: (877) 426-8056,
Fax (877) 426-2166
Web: http://www.elderhostel.org/
Education and travel organization for adults 55 and over.

Ingrid Boesel
Fiberworks
27 Suffolk St W,
Guelph, Ontario,
N1H 2H9, Canada
Tel: (519) 822-5988
Fax: (519) 822-3095
Web: http://www.fiberworks-pcw.com/
Uses workshops and lectures to teach about designing complex weaves such as Inspiration from Your Fabric Store; and Images and Ties. Also Fiberworks PCW software.

Sharon Marcus
Portland, OR
Email: smmarcus@compuserve.com
Tapestry artist, presents lectures and workshops on design: Finding the Contemporary in the Historic; Get Serious: Design a Series; Ways of Working; Master Class: Focusing and Refining Your Work; Pushing Your Ideas Further - A Mixed Media Approach to Design; Inspiration from the Sciences.

Chapter 5

New World Textiles
PO Box 1484
Black Mountain, NC 28711
Tel: (828) 669-1870
Web: http://buncombe.main.nc.us/~ehallman
20/2 unmercerized cotton, natural colored cotton, spinning fibers and equipment

Ann Johnston
P. O. Box 944
Lake Oswego, OR 97034
Tel: (800) 247-6553
Fax: (419) 281-6883
Web: www.annjohnston.net
order@bookmaster.com
Books on dye painting and design

Chapter 6

Kopykake
3699 W. 240th St.
Torrance, CA 90505
Tel: (310) 373-8906
Toll free: (800) 999-5253
Fax: (310) 375-5275
Web: http://www.kopykake.com/home.html
Copy projectors for enlarging or reducing designs

The Singing Weaver
Web: www.singingweaver.com
48” wide non-fusible featherweight interfacing for cartoons
#17 gauge curved mattress needles for stitching at the loom
Warping On a Shoestring 20-page booklet
Warping On a Shoestring 39-minute video

Daniel Smith Fine Artists' Materials
4150 First Ave. South
Seattle, WA 98134-2302
Tel: (800) 426-6740
Web: http://www.danielsmith.com/
Permacolor® art markers and other art supplies

Pyramid School Products
6510 North 54th Street
Tampa, FL 33610
Phone: (813) 621-6446
Toll Free: (800) 792-2644
Fax: (813) 621-7688
Web: http://www.lifeisart.com/art-supplies.htm
Permacolor® art markers and other art supplies

Macomber Looms
PO Box 186
Beech Ridge Road
York, ME 03909
Tel: (207) 363-2808

Fiber Arts School and Gallery
2060 West La Habra Blvd.
La Habra, CA 90532
Tel: (562) 691-1016
Workshops, ongoing classes, fiber gallery

Acclaimed Quilt Displays
P.O. Box 54289
Cincinnati, OH 45254
Tel: (888) 487-7233
Web: http://www.displayaway.com/
DisplayAway™ hanging devices for textiles

Chapter 7

Handwoven
Interweave Press
201 E. Fourth St.
Loveland, CO 80537-5655.
Tel: (800) 272-2194
http://www.interweave.com/weave/

Tessellation
Here are some places to start learning about tessellations and M.C. Escher.
http://www.worldofescher.com/
http://mathforum.org/sum95/suzanne/links.html

Knots on The Web
http://www.earlham.edu/~peters/knotlink.html
http://www.learn2.com/05/0540/0540.asp
Knot web sites

Chapter 8

Hoffman Fabrics California-International
25792 Obrero Drive
Mission Viejo, CA 92691
Tel: (800) 547-0100
Fax: (949) 770-4022
Web: http://www.hoffmanfabrics.com/quilt-gallery.html

Chapter 9

Karen Noe Design
Søndergade 23
DK-7171 Uldum
Denmark
Tel: +45 7567 9733
Fax +45 7567 9833
Web: http://www.karen-noe.dk/index.html
Email: noe@karen-noe.dk
Patterns and yarns for knitting and weaving, buttons, dyes

The Singing Weaver
Web: www.singingweaver.com
Patterns: Thai Jacket Pattern, Mondrian Vest Pattern, Six-Panel Jacket

Yarn Barn
930 Massachusetts
Lawrence, KS 66044
Tel: (785) 842-4333
Orders: (800) 468-0035
Fax: (785) 842-0794
Web: http://www.yarnbarn-ks.com/
Jaggerspun, UKI, Harrisville yarns

Herrschners, Inc.
2800 Hoover Road
Stevens Point, WI 54492 Tel: (800) 441-0838
Fax: (715) 341-2250
Web: http://www.dmc-usa.com/
DMC floss and pearl cotton

UKI Supreme Corporation
PO Box 1656
Hickory, NC 28603
Tel: (704) 322-6975
Toll free: (888) 604-6975
Fax: (704) 322-7881
Email: uki@ukisupreme.com
Cotton yarn

SouthStar Supply Company
Nashville, TN
Tel: (615) 353-7000
Toll Free: (800) 288-6739
Fax: (615) 353-7155
Toll Free: (800) 842-7358
Web: http://www.southstarsupply.com/
Sussman Pressmaster irons

Linda Kubik
310 East 8th Ave
Ritzville, WA 99169
Tel: (509) 659-0209
Fax: (509) 659-1913
Web: www.kubikelements.com
Interfacings, Elements Patterns

Chapter 10

Pendleton Woolen Mills
Portland, OR
Tel: (800) 760-4844
Web: http://www.pendleton-usa.com/

Fibonacci series is formed by adding the latest two numbers to get the next one, starting from 0 and 1:
Web site directory to numerous sites on Fibonacci.
http://www.mcs.surrey.ac.uk/Personal/R.Knott/Fibonacci/fib.html

Cougar Wright Crossing Press
Cheryl Samuels
PO Box 665
Sangudo, Alberta T0E 2A0
Canada
Web: www.ravenstail.com
A series of workbooks on Celtic Line Drawing

Halcyon Yarn
12 School Street
Bath, Maine 04530
Tel: (207) 442-7909
Toll Free: (800) 341-0282
Fax (207) 442-0633
Web: http://www.halcyonyarn.com/
Reynold's Icelandic Yarn (Lopi)

HeartStrings
Jackie Erickson-Schweitzer
53 Parlange Drive
Destrehan, LA 70047-2133
Tel: (985) 764-8094
Toll free: (888) 955-8094
Web: http://www.heartstringsfiberarts.com/
Klippan Swedish Matt Garn

Shannock Tapestry Looms
PO Box 65295
Vancouver, WA 98665
Tel: (360) 573-7264
Fax: (360) 573-0384
http://www.shannocklooms.com/
Cotton seine twine, linen

Pro Chemical and Dye
P.O. Box 14
Somerset, MA 02726
Orders: (800) 228 9393
Technical Support: (508) 676-3838
Fax: (509) 676-3980
Web: http://www.prochemical.com/
Dye supplies

Mary Zicafoose
Tel: (402) 344-1589
Web:
http://fiberartists.org/gallery/mary_zicafoose/
Email: kirbyzic@ix.netcome.com
Designer, weaver and teacher of weft ikat

Chapter 11

American Quilter's Society
P.O. Box 3290
Paducah, KY 42002-3290
Tel: (270) 898-7903
Orders: (800) 626-5420
Fax: (270) 898-1173
Web: http://www.aqsquilt.com/
AQS Show, annual event in April

International Quilt Association
7660 Woodway, Suite 550
Houston, TX 77063
Tel: (713) 781-6864
Fax: (713) 781-8182
Web: http://www.quilts.org/
Houston International Quilt Festival, annual event in November

Ornament Inc.
P.O. Box 2349
San Marcos, CA 92079
Tel: (760) 599-0222
Fax: (760) 599-0228
Ornament Magazine

Stampington and Company
22992 Mill Creek, Suite B
Laguna Hills, CA 92653
Tel: (949) 380-7318
Toll free: (877) 782-6737
Fax: (949) 380-9355
Web: http://www.stampington.com/
Belle Armoire Art to Wear magazine

Boeing Surplus Sales
South 208th St and 84 Ave South
Kent, WA
Tel: (425) 393-4065

Toray America Inc.
Web: http://www.ultrasuede.com/home/
Ultrasuede fabric and information

General Resources and additional chapter related resources are listed on the CD-ROM.

Index

Graphics Credits

All photography not otherwise credited is by Kim Sheagren.
All illustrations not otherwise credited are by Marie Westerman.
All other drafts and scans not otherwise credited are by Adam Brusic.
Cover design by Kim Sheagren.

Other credits are as follows: p. vi Deborah Elliott; p. 4 Nadine Sanders; p. 7 Nadine Sanders; p.15 Neal Olson; p.16 Joyce Harter; p. 17 Neal Olson; p. 23 photographer unknown (National Geographic); p. 24 drawings by Nadine Sanders; p. 25 drawings and collage by Joyce Harter; p. 26 collage by Nadine Sanders; watercolor by Joyce Harter; p. 28 drawing by Nadine Sanders; p. 28 Joyce Harter (left); p. 29 postcard image reproduced from a painting by Carl Larsson; wrappings by Nadine Sanders; p. 31 Fred Gonnerman; p. 33 Fred Gonnerman (bottom); p. 37 Patricia Kraus; Joyce Harter; p. 41 Neal Olson; p. 42 Joyce Harter; p. 44 Nadine Sanders (bottom); p. 45 used by permission of Eileen Chadwick; p. 53 Mount Burns (left) p. 58-59 Nadine Sanders; p. 67 Stan Giske (left), Larry Hoffman (right); p. 85 Joyce Harter; p. 95 Nadine Sanders; p. 98 Nadine Sanders; p. 99 Nadine Sanders (left), Mount Burns (right); p.100 Mount Burns; p.103 drawing by workshop student, photo by Nadine Sanders; p. 104-105 Peter Horsfall.

The CD-ROM is an ever-changing, expanding partner to this book. A CD-ROM table of contents will be added to the book as an insert page as the accompanying disk is updated.